Visualizing Is
Realizing

Also by Mark Victor Hansen

BOOKS

Chicken Soup for the Soul series—254 different books in print

The One Minute Millionaire

Cracking the Millionaire Code

Cash in a Flash

How to Make the Rest of Your Life the Best of Your Life

The Aladdin Factor

Dare to Win

The Richest Kids in America

The Miracle of Tithing

The Power of Focus

The Miracles in You

Out of the Blue

Master Motivator

You Are the Solution

You Have a Book in You

Speed Write Your Personal Life Story

Speed Write Your First Fiction Book

Speed Write Your Nonfiction Book

Speed Write Your Mega Book Marketing Plan

Speed Write Your First Screenplay

Speed Write (and Deliver) Your Killer Speech

Speed Write Your Amazing Publishing Plan

Speed Edit Your First Book

Visualizing is Realizing

Dreams Don't Have Deadlines

AUDIOS

How to Think Bigger than You Ever Thought You Could Think

Dreams Don't Have Deadlines

Visualizing Is Realizing

Sell Yourself Rich

Chicken Soup for the Soul series

The One Minute Millionaire

Cracking the Millionaire Code

Visualizing is Realizing

What You See is
What You Get

Mark Victor Hansen

MEDIA

Published 2020 by Gildan Media LLC
aka G&D Media
www.GandDmedia.com

Front Cover design by David Rheinhardt of Pyrographx

Interior design by Meghan Day Healey of Story Horse, LLC

Library of Congress Cataloging-in-Publication Data is available upon request

ISBN: 978-1-7225-0315-4

10 9 8 7 6 5 4 3 2 1

I visualized my ideal woman to be my soul mate. Crystal, you realized all 267-plus written dreams and more, becoming more than I visualized or imagined— you are my beloved twin flame.

Contents

Preface

You have the enormous power to visualize to realize your heartfelt dreams, hopes, prayers, and desires. Visualizing is a God-given gift that is hidden you inside you from birth. You have to become aware of this inward talent and resource and to learn how to use it. It behooves you to practice visualizing your life to perfection in order to realize every good thing that you have ever desired.

Visualizing has magical, mystical, and proven abilities to help you:

- Realize your destiny.
- Know that the best will happen to and for you.
- Fulfill your most exciting visions for what's possible.

- Awaken to abundance, riches, and unlimited wealth.
- Heal you from sickness, disease, and pain.
- Help you discover the love of your life.
- Work at your right livelihood.
- Raise you from poverty to prosperity and abundance.
- Build unstoppable self-confidence, self-esteem, and self-worth in you.
- Find your true love and romance.
- Rise to unimaginable heights of success, achievement, and happiness.
- Experience and express breakthrough freedom, opportunities, and increases.
- Orchestrate an extraordinary life worth living.
- Stimulate the possibilities for you to go further and faster in life.
- Give you a second or third chance.
- Overcome your fear, doubt, anxieties, and worries.
- Give you leadership abilities.
- Manifest new perspectives.
- Help you learn, earn, and return vastly more.
- Discover explosive blessings.
- Live longer, with a higher quality of life and living.

- Become a person of respect and renown—a record maker.
- Leave a historical legacy worthy of you.
- Increase your capacity to receive and give.
- Make your journey through life worthwhile, fun, and joyously impactful.
- See that the world has yeses in your future.

After going bankrupt in 1974 and feeling trashed, unworthy of life, and generally useless, I started reading and studying self-help books, listening endlessly to positively motivational audios, attending positive thinking churches, and attending uplifting and inspiring lectures. My life dramatically changed for the better.

Before that time, I had never heard about visualization as a technique. Suddenly I saw it used by every superstar in business, writing, sports, ministry, politics, and life. Wow! Once I learned it, my earnings skyrocketed. My life force energy returned. I became a happy, healthy, contributing member of the human race again. My life improved in every way and has relentlessly continued to do so. I am proud to have learned that visualizing is realizing.

I am excited to share these life transforming principles with you now. When we meet, I want to hear your story of dramatic and exciting transformation and realization through visualization.

May this book inspire you in the depth of your soul to master visualizing in order to live a life of health, wealth, happiness, and abundance in all areas. May I congratulate you in advance as you proceed to exceed your expectations on this wondrous journey.

Happy reading!

Mark Victor Hansen
Scottsdale, Arizona
September 2020

Note: This book is also available as an audio book by the same name.

The Principles of Creative Visualization

- Begin with your feeling nature.
- Relaxed awakeness.
- Controlled reverie.
- Come from the end result.

One

Who Creates Your Life?

Who creates your life?

You do.

The good news is that you can create it to be as wonderful, as magnificent, joyous, and treasure-filled as you like. The mind says that whatever you're ready for is ready for you.

That readiness, the preparation state of the mind, is 87 percent visually oriented. Webster says that visualization is the mental imagery of the mind. Whatever picture you put in your mind is what's going to show up. What you impress, you express. If you get into the highest level, the depth of your inner being, your every mental impression becomes an expression. You get into what psychologist Dr. Jean Houston calls the sacred psychology of the human mind, because you live full-time in your own human biocomputer. It can either be heaven in there or hell.

Who's at choice?

You are.

Once you start playing with the tissue of your mind and you understand that what you impress, you express, you can ask yourself whether you want to play with the best or the worst.

If you're going to play the game, why not play with the best that exists?

If you play with the best, it creates more of the best. When you're playing with the stuff of mind tissue, you start sculpting it with your inner eye and say, "How would it look if it was marvelous? How would it look if it was perfect?"

As Christ said, "It will be done according to you according to your belief." Your real belief is what manifests in your life, so if you've got sickness in your life, it's because you've got sick thoughts. If you've got health in your life, you've got healthy thoughts. Your imagination creates your reality.

If you can be successful fast or slowly, which way do you want to go?

If it can be easy or hard, which way do you want to do it?

The answer is obvious, isn't it? Isn't that what Christ said? "My yoke is easy, and my burden is light" (Matthew 11:30). It's not the weather that should determine your reality. It's your mental state, because your state of mind creates your results.

Who owns your state of mind?

You do.

One person can make a difference if they see themselves making a difference. Can you see yourself making a difference?

Punch through Your Doubts

The minute you decide to take a stand and make a difference, are you going to get attacked?

Yes. And the first things that are going to attack you are your own doubt thoughts. "You never did that before; what makes you think you can do it now? Who the heck do you think you are?" Most of us keep unconsciously reiterating everything we've heard, which maintains the pattern of our lives.

Your body is a pattern in integrity. If you are over twenty-five years old, you have taken in over a million pounds of food, but you don't weigh a million pounds (thank God!). It comes in and goes out. There's a magical flow. There's an ingress and an egress.

This pattern in integrity *is* you, but it's set up in the higher dimensions of mind. This has to do with sacred psychology, which goes beyond the ordinary plebeian psychologies. At the beginning of the twentieth century, the great psychologist and philosopher William James said, "Parted from us by the flimsiest of screens are realities that you can't even suspect until you punch through them."

Where will you punch through them? At the level of mind, what you think about comes about, and it comes in an affirmative state. What we're really looking for is *ahas*.

I've already mentioned Dr. Jean Houston, who I would say is the grand master of visualization. Her father was one of the head humor writers for Bob Hope. As a girl, she was always getting in trouble with the Catholic church because her mind was so expansive.

Jean used to go for walks in Central Park, and almost daily she would run into a wonderful snow-haired man who just talked to her. She didn't learn his name at first, but he turned out to be the great anthropologist and theologian Pierre Teilhard de Chardin.

Can you imagine a little seven-year-old walking her dog, getting to talk with Teilhard de Chardin, and learning about what he called the "phenomenon of man"? Later somebody gave her one of his books, and she said, "That's my best friend. That's the guy I've spent my conscious time thinking with." Anyhow, she does the cosmic dance of life as well as anyone else, and she takes people through the process of sacred psychology.

Here's what Jean Houston says: visualization facilitates mental imaging and effective thought generation. I'd add that it'll also give you the facility to regenerate thought. It allows you to return to your spiritual source, so you can search for the beloved of your soul.

Where is the real place to find love? Inside or outside?

Inside. It's your own home entertainment center, and it could be the most exquisite place to live. The teacher of my teacher, R. Buckminster Fuller, was Albert Einstein. I love this story about Einstein: He's walking across the Princeton campus one day. A young student walks up and says, "Professor, can I ask you a question?"

"Anything," he says. He answers it laboriously for about an hour and a half. At the end, Einstein says, "Young man, can I ask you a question?"

"What is it?"

"When we got together, was I going this way or that way?"

"Professor, you were going that way. Why do you ask?"

"Good. Then I've had breakfast."

Bucky Fuller said that the first time he met Einstein, he just glowed. Why? Because he was a very high-consciousness individual. His head lived in the stars, or in the universe. Maybe he didn't have the right accoutrements or sartorial splendor, but his emanations were those of the high states of consciousness, high states of cosmology and cosmogony. I'm going to talk about some of these in this book.

Now say aloud, "One, one, one, one, one, one, one, one." It's a form of meditation that anyone can do, and after a couple of times you're likely feel a transcendent experience. The reason is that you get out of normal day-to-day thinking and uplevel yourself with one meditative mantra.

Isn't that fun? Jean says it will allow you to extend your body. I have watched as Jean has hypnotized a nonmusical nun to play Mozart's *Unfinished Concerto*, so there is vast unrealized and unexplored potential in each of us. Visualization is one of the avenues that grants us access into higher dimensions of our own mind.

In Orange County, California, there is a seven-year-old kid that I've watched. He can put his feet on top of a book and read that book for you as well as you can with physical sight, and he is totally blind. These technologies, methodologies, and potentialities have existed for a long time.

A lot of people say, "That's woo-wee stuff." It's not. Your body is not limited to your physicality unless your *mind* is limited to your physicality. The trouble is, we've grown to think that we are, but we're not. I'm more than my physicality. More than my mentality. We have been given the ability to create and contribute, using our free will that was given to us (see Genesis 1:27–28).

Touch yourself right now and say, *I am more than my physicality. I am more than my mentality. I am God's greatest masterpiece* (see Ephesians 2:10).

If you're more than who you think you are, you can do all sorts of wonderful things. The first time I learned how to extend myself out of my body, I was in India. I had amoebic dysentery. A little guru visiting with me was teaching me how to have out-of-body experiences, and he said, "My dear man, if you don't want to feel the pain, you transfer it out of your body. You say, 'Why don't I take it and put it two feet out of my body?' You'll spend the rest of the morning putting the pain two feet out of your body, and you won't feel it any more."

"Thank God," I said, "because I think I'm going to die if it stays."

I learned how to take that pain and put it out of my body. You can do lots of stuff. But what do most people do if they've got pains? They want to talk about them. They want to reiterate them. They say, "Oh, my ache. Oh, my God. It's so bad. You don't know how bad it is," and they get their payoff by talking about their pain. What do they get? They get more pain.

Why not focus on something else? Your mind can only think one thought at a time (although it can think quite a few in relatively rapid sequence), so limit your thought to "I am pain-free." If you don't like the situation you are in, put yourself in a situation that you would like by visualizing it, by living in the feeling and assumption of your wish fulfilled.

A while ago, I was flying across country. I had as my seatmate Nobel prize winner Dr. Milton Friedman, chairman of the economics department at the University of Chicago. We got into some extremely turbulent air. We were sitting up in front, where you get less rocking, but that didn't help any.

The plane was jumping up and down, and it made me believe in the terra firma—the more firma, the less terror. That thing was doing wave pulsation at 200 and 300 feet at a shot, and it was scaring me.

I turned to Friedman and said, "Look, my dear friend. You can only think one thought at a time."

"I've never heard that. Are you sure?"

"You can think a lot of thoughts in sequence, but the mind is an nonsimultaneous mechanism: you can only think one thought at a time. Therefore let's think about something other than regurgitating or getting sick."

At that time, Friedman was the economic advisor to Ronald Reagan. He said, "The interesting thing here is that when I talk, you take notes. When you talk, I take notes. When I talk at the university, everybody takes notes. But when I go in to talk to the president, he's the only guy that doesn't take notes. It unnerves me a little bit. I get to talk to him for seven, nine, or twelve minutes. An amazing thing is he's got twenty-two other advisers that come in every Monday, laying down the way the world works, and somehow he integrates all that himself. He doesn't take notes, there is no tape recorder, and nobody else is in there with us. The guy's got an incredible mind. He has learned how to have perfect retention."

"What do you think about that?" I asked. "Did you ever ask him?"

"Yeah," he said, "He programs himself to perfect retention of what he wants."

Right now, touch yourself and say, *I've got perfect retention of what I want. That's perfected visualization to realization.*

After all, you don't want to remember the bad stuff. That's why women who have gone through childbirth do not remember the pain of labor; otherwise they would not do it twice. (As the famous comedian Carol Burnett has said, if men want to know how painful childbirth is, they should take their lower lip and stretch it up over the top of their head.)

You Have Greatness in You

Genius gives you an amplified mind. Why operate with a plebeian mind? Our school system says we have to have everybody learn exactly the same things. That is an asinine model.

Once I addressed a gathering of school principals in California. I was not being critical of them; I was being critical of the system. They gave me a fifteen-minute standing ovation. Then they hired me to do six different major projects, one of which was to get the unrepresented students, such as Indians, Hispanics, and blacks, represented in the system. I said, "H. Ross Perot is one of the five great heroes in America right now, and he's using amplified mind power. He's figured out how to pay teachers $100,000 each down in Texas to be great and inspiring."

We don't need garbage teachers. We need great, inspiring teachers. Every one of us needs to operate at our highest, best, noblest, and most important levels. Greatness is intrinsic within us.

Right now, jab yourself in the chest and say, *I've got greatness in me.*

It's when you start claiming that you're great that you get tuned in and turned on to your highest and best. It's what Paul said, "Think on these things—the things that are noble, lovely, beautiful, and of good report" (Philippians 4:8). That's when the mind wakes up.

That's when you unzip the old and you let it go just as a snake gets rid of the old skin.

Right now, pretend that you have a zipper from your crown of your head, called in India your crown chakra or energy zone, and take it right down to your crotch. Imagine yourself zipping off the old skin, like a snake. Say, *I'm zipping off the old, and I'm taking it off right now. I'm leaving it here, and I'm not picking it up. And I've got a shiny, bright exterior and interior. I sparkle. I'm repletely and completely beautiful. I know that I know that I know. I am the new me.*

That's the point of having an amplified mind. I've mentioned H. Ross Perot. When he was working with IBM in 1962, he sold his annual quota in the first nineteen days. IBM, which wasn't programmed right at that juncture, said, "Good. You're retired for the rest of the year."

For God's sake! When somebody is productive and creative and resourceful and hits their goals, what do you do? Don't retire them. Give them bigger goals.

Perot said, "Look. If you guys won't let me work and you're going to pay me, then I'll create my own company."

They said, "If you think you can do that, go do it."

Perot started Electronic Data Systems (EDS). He called on eighty people to help him, and they all said no.

Now most people quit the first time they hear no. When my hero, Thomas Alva Edison, was interviewed by inspirational author Napoleon Hill, Hill said, "My God, my man, you failed ten thousand times."

Edison said, "Whoa. I never failed. I had ten thousand learning experiences. I ran out of ways that wouldn't work. I finally had to find a way that it would." That's the principle we're looking for.

The eighty-first person Perot called on was Governor Nelson Rockefeller, who bought Perot's model the first time he heard it. That was a gross sale of $4 million. Divide $8 million by 80 calls, and you see that Perot got paid the equivalent of $50,000 for every time he heard no and his thoughtful proposal was rejected. Perot told me he could see it in his mind and worked to realize it with self-disciplined action to achieve a result. Later he sold the company to GM (General Motors) for $2.5 billion. Visualization means metaphorically creating the acorn of what you desire and in your mind seeing it grow into a giant oak tree—in Perot's case a future multibillion-dollar acquisition.

Note: my definition of an entrepreneur is someone who solves a problem for a vast profit. Perot was a perfect entrepreneur who used his brilliant problem solving abilities for many outcomes, as we will continue to discuss.

What did Perot sell? He sold the concept. Where was it? In his mind. The point is, if anyone can have great concepts, everyone can.

So Perot started EDS and did exceedingly well. At one point, he had people in Iran. After the revolution there, when the Ayatollah Khomeini came to power, they put two of Perot's people in the slammer. At that time we had a government that was ineffectual in getting back prisoners, so Perot had a masterful idea. He said, "I'm going to get with the best guy that can get this done." He got a former Army colonel, Arthur "Bull" Simons, who led a 1970 raid on a POW camp in North Vietnam.

Perot went over there himself. Bull Simons said, "Look. You're a billionaire. You don't need to do this."

"It's not a question of need," Perot said. "I want to. I'm the guy who put those people at risk. I'm the one who has the obligation. They were working for me. They were an extension of what my dream was, and as long as they're in prison, I've got to do everything within my power to get them out."

He sprang not only his own prisoners but all the others who were in the same prison. Ken Follett tells the story in his book *Wings of Eagles*, which was made into a movie.

Do you have a friend who would do that for you? Do you have one friend that you could call right now who would give you $5,000, $100,000, or whatever your giant need is (God forbid you should need it)?

I've written a fair number of coauthored books and plan to do a whole lot more, because it leverages me and gets things done in a nanosecond, because, as I said, if you have the choice of doing it fast or slow, you want to do it fast.

I cowrote a book with Don Dible, who also wrote the best seller *Up Your Own Organization*. One morning we were sitting at breakfast and said, "How can we make each other a million dollars?"

We decided do a book series called *Build a Better You Starting Now*, and it went wondrously well.

Then Don went into the seminar business. Unfortunately he hit a glitch in the road. One day he went bankrupt, with 11,000 creditors. He went down for $10 million.

Because a lot of people knew that he and I are close friends, they called and said, "I hope you're not going down with him."

"What a bizarre thing to say," I thought. Here's the principle, though: good news travels fast; bad news travels faster.

I called Don Dible, because I'd gone bankrupt myself. I told him, "I understand the pain and anguish and torment you're going through. They're going to go for your jugular. They're going to take every ounce of your spirit away from you in a very short time.

"Because of my love and affection for you, I don't want anything from you, but I want to serve you this way. I'd like you, your wife, Allison, and your son, Max, to be our houseguests this weekend. Don't give the phone number to anyone else, especially your attorney, because if they can't get you, they're going to go for him, and he's going to go back to you. Two weeks from now—I've already bought your tickets—we're taking you to our condo in Hawaii. I just want you to have a place to rest and relax."

In my book *Dare to Win*, I point out that when your self-worth goes up, your net worth goes up.

The danger is that when your net worth goes down, we let our self-worth go down.

I'm not bragging about myself in this story. I'm asking, do you have a terrific friend who, if, God forbid, you're in the wrong place at the wrong time, will support you even before you ask? As the verse in Isaiah says, "Before you ask, I will have answered" (Isaiah 65:24), assuming you're asking rightly.

Integrating Head and Heart

All of this comes out of amplified mind, which will give you a compassionate heart. When we make a hard decision, our head says, "No. That's not a good idea. It's going to come back on you superbad, baby." When you're doing your head stuff, you think with your wallet. You figure out what you *can't* do rather than on what you *can* do. As long as you're figuring out what you can't do, you won't do it. You need to figure out how your heart is and integrate it with your head. That's why the Bible says, "As a man thinketh in his heart, so is he" (Proverbs 23:7).

When a lot of people study metaphysics, they think, "I can just trip out on the head stuff, and it's going to be wonderful." It isn't. The goal is to operate from your heart, your heart chakra, your heart energy zone and then take massive action in the right direction.

The inspirational preacher Reverend Ike used to say, "Let your *fulfeelment* precede your *fulfillment* by being full of *fulthrillment*," meaning, get thrilled and excited about whatever you want in advance of having it. Then you'll vibrationally synchronize in time and space with the good that you desire, which you do in visualization. You have to expectantly and feelingly believe that it is true before it is actually and tangibly true. The subconscious cannot tell the difference between imagined reality and reality, but it acts on the feeling nature of your belief. So what you deeply and fervently impress you will ultimately and inevitably express.

Later I'm going to describe the inner steps of visualization. One is, where is your feeling nature? When people don't have enough money, many of them say, "Oh my God, I'm going to go bankrupt. They're going to take out the telephone, take away my credit cards, repossess my car, and bankrupt me. They're going to foreclose on the house. They're going to take back my clothes from Nordstrom's when I can't pay my bills."

If you plan on that and you keep studying it, that's what shows up. Why? The subconscious is neutral. In the Sermon on the Mount, Jesus says, God "maketh his sun to rise on the evil and on the good" (Matthew 5:45). The subconscious doesn't care. "There is no respect of persons with God," as it says in Romans 2:11. God loves you no matter what. But you are here, and you are the cocreator of your good. Therefore you're at freedom either to screw it up or to make it wonderful.

Right now, touch yourself and inwardly declare, *I'm at choice. I choose to make my life and lifestyle a masterpiece. Others have come back from the brink of disaster and succeeded extravagantly, and so will I!*

When you have a compassionate heart, who's the first one you got to have compassion to and for? You. You are the world's foremost authority on you. You must positively and correctly love yourself, enhance your self-esteem and self-worth, and grow to realize your fullest potential in all areas of your life. You are a human becoming and forever becoming more, if and only if you choose to become all you are capable of being. There is more in you!

Now say, *I love me real good.*

As my late friend Dr. Leo Buscaglia, author of the best-selling book *Love*, used to say, "You're the only sweet old self you get to be with." If you're going to give to yourself, give yourself the best.

Now touch yourself and say, *I'm giving myself the best.*

When you give *you* the best, you can give the world the best. We've got to have individual and personal transformation before we can get world transformation. Whatever you've got inside and you're picturizing is going to show up one way or another outside. Choose positive, uplifting, and beneficent images to cogitate, ruminate, and meditate on.

You're just the right person to read this book. You're the one that needs or wants this. And I'm the one that can give you what want you want (or at least that's what I hope). It'll build a more active soul for both of us. As Jean Houston says, "It'll create a high life of service." You are here for two C's—to *create* and to *contribute*. Visualization is the front end of mastering your abilities of creating and contributing massively and impactfully. Mother Teresa believed, visualized, and said: "With three cents and God, I can do anything." She single-handedly inspired the world, lifting many out of poverty while attracting enormous amounts in charity through her profound visualizations and eloquent communications to audiences worldwide.

You might be saying, "Wait a second. I don't want to be into service. I want to relax. I want a vacation. I want to cool it." It's OK to cool it. If it fits you, I would like you to take three months of every year off, but don't retire, because if you retire too early, you expire in one year. Florida is called America's graveyard because 12 percent of the population dies there.

Jean also says that in sacred psychology, you become a citizen larger than your aspiration and more complex than all your dreams. See, here's the deal. If you don't do your own dreaming, then somebody else will, and there's a serious danger to that. If you don't dream for yourself, then somebody who's got a bigger dream than you, which you accept, casts an enchantment. They'll lay their deal on you rather than letting you have your own deal. I want to inspire you to be an innovative, omniprofitable capitalist. You have to visualize that to realize it. I know it is better to be rich than poor. I have been both. Rich is in every way better. I did it by visualizing myself to where I am, and you can too. Like goal setting, it costs no money, but you have to put in the desire, energy, and daily discipline to achieve your heart's desires.

Let me use an easily understandable example. You are at a restaurant with four or five people. There is one person at the head of the table, the person who has the most eminence. Whether this person is male or female is irrelevant. The waiter will come to that person and ask, "What do you want?"

Whatever that person says, everybody else will say, "I'll have that." Have you ever seen that? Why? The person at the head of the table wasn't laying it on the others; they just hadn't thought through their own choices.

Jab yourself in the chest and say, *If I'm at choice—and I am—I'm making my own decisions, and they are really good.*

In his best-selling book *Jonathan Livingston Seagull,* Richard Bach says, "Create things; don't just compete."

There's only one person to compete with, and who's that?

Yourself.

At the level of the human mind, everybody is born rich. We're born with 86 billion brain cells or whatever scientists can actually count. The fact is that we are all endowed with seeds of greatness, brilliance, skills and talents—beyond what we are using. They come to work when you decide to make use of them.

Consciousness makes the decision, which implodes into the subconscious. The subconscious is always out picturing whatever you've been in-picturing. What you deeply impress in your mind and heart, you will express in your life and experience.

Here's the deal. The conscious mind is inductive: it goes from the specific to the general. By contrast, the subconscious is deductive: it goes from general to specific. If you say, "I'm healthy," your subconscious figures out how to attract to you the people that tell you how to become healthy. If you say, "I'm rich," your subconscious is going to figure out how to make you rich.

These are the vehicles you're going to use. I would suggest that you plan on using multiple vehicles. Why? Because everything pulsates and vibrates in the universe. Everything has a rhythmic and circadian flow to it. Therefore if you're in the wrong flow, something else will be in the right flow; it doesn't matter, because there's pattern in integrity. Although we teach the concept of cause and effect, the universe is actually multi-causal.

I recommend that you watch the movie *Gandhi*, about Mahatma Gandhi. *Mahatma* means *great spirit*. Here was a guy with an idea that united India's population—450 million at the time. He was well-educated, there's no question about that, but he had no media, no army. Yet he got the people together to win independence and freedom just by doing freedom walks and salt marches.

Richard Attenborough, the director of the film, was so intrigued with this idea that he had written the script twenty years before. Why couldn't he do it earlier? Because Ben Kingsley, the actor who magnificently portrayed Gandhi and won an Academy Award for it, was only eight years old at the time. There is a perfect time and season for everything. I have a set of audios called *Dreams Don't Have Deadlines*.

The inspirational preacher Robert Schuller had a great line about this: "God's delays are not God's denials." Sometimes you get the go sign. Sometimes you get the stop sign. The stop sign isn't bad, but if you're impatient, if you're a type A or if, like me, you're a triple A, you've got to keep your mojo moving. That's why I take so much time in Hawaii. I take six weeks off, and pretty soon I'll be up to three months, because it cools me out to be in a mecca where I don't accept telephone calls. I'm in heaven, just floating around in my pool or windsurfing on the Pacific Ocean.

Do you need to reduce your stress? The late psychologist Dr. Hans Selye formulated the concept of *eustress* (from the Greek adverb *eu*, which means *well* or *good*). It's good stress, compared to *distress*, which is the bad kind. There's the stress of normal living, and then there's distress, which comes from having too much all at once.

Visualize Right Livelihood

To get out of prison, you must first be aware that you're in one. A lot of us are in the prison of a limited reality. You say, "I don't know if I could do any better. I don't know if I can go any further in this job." If you can't, then it's time to get out.

You may say, "You don't understand. I've got to feed myself. I've got to feed the kids. I don't know if I can do it." In Hebrews 11:1, it says, "Faith is the substance of things unseen." Faith is substance. That means you've got to have it before you get it. Faith is a state of mind. You've only got two states of mind: faith and fear. Most of us are used to hovering around fear: "Oh my God. I am going to blow it. If I leave this secure job, what will they think?"

For example, I had a relative say, "What I really want to do is go down to Florida and get a fishing boat. I want to make my living by renting out time on the boat. That's what I'm going to do after I retire."

"You don't have to wait," I said.

"Why not?"

"I have a friend who does all the insurance for boats up and down the whole eastern coast of Florida. I'll just have him find a deal."

"Oh, you can't do that."

Because of his limited reality, he assumed that I couldn't deliver on my promise. A lot of us live in a limited reality: "I can't dance, so I'm going to be a wallflower." That isn't the program. It doesn't matter if you can dance well; just do it. Emerson said, "Do the thing, and you have the power."

I called up my friend in insurance and said, "I've got a relative who wants to be into the business of taking people out fishing. Is there any way you can find somebody that's ready to retire and wants to sell his boat?"

Within an hour, he called back, said, "This guy, who's eighty-one, will sell his." He would do a leveraged buyout or a no-cash-down deal.

I called up my relative and said, "I've got the program."

"Oh no," he said. "You're kidding. I can't do that."

"*Excusez-moi*," I said. "I'd swear that I'd heard you say that this is what you want to do after retirement and that you'd love to do it now, but you didn't see a way. You didn't see that somebody could part the screen for you, go to the other side, then bring it back to you."

"No, I can't do that."

"Why not?"

"I get retirement in thirteen more years."

"Wait a second. You told me you hate what you're doing. You can't stand going there." He was head of a nuclear power plant in the Midwest. He got there inadvertently and did not want to be there. "Look," I said. "I teach that you shouldn't spend one second doing something you completely hate, because all your life is made of is exalted seconds."

What am I trying to do here? I'm trying to pique your interest in stabbing your spirit alive and waking up to becoming what you can be, because if all of us become our highest and best, we make space for those behind us. We clear the way for street people who don't want to be in the street. They don't smell good enough or look good enough, so they went for jobs and got turned down enough that they shut themselves down. They are locked into a limited reality, but as we go higher, we can get others out of limited realities.

I was trying to help my relative get out of a limited reality, but he said, "I can't do that." See, every cause has an effect. His causal thought was that "I've got to hang out until I get this retirement." I can't imagine that—thirteen years of doing something that disgusts you, that is repugnant to you, that you resist and resent. Yet once I read in *Newsweek* that 85 percent of the people are dissatisfied with their jobs. Why be dissatisfied with your job? Why not visualize your right livelihood and then create it?

Right now, say, "I'm visualizing my right livelihood, and I'm creating it, right here, and right now."

Two

New Spaces of Possibility

What I've just done is wake up some of your consciousness. As you read this, you can see that these things are now new possibilities.

We're creating new spaces of possibility. We're amplifying your thinking. Many of us need to get out of the prison of a limited reality. A lot of people say, "The poor will always be with you." That is bunk. It is time to get rid of the limited belief that because we've never fed all of humanity, doesn't mean that we can't. Today we have the resources, people, and agricultural breakthroughs to bring in excess food production. We have vast supply chains wanting to profitably deliver even more food. We have technology that can grow food in a greenhouse under the green- and red-light spectrum in half the time. We can cost-effectively produce water directly out of the air by condensation, like Zero Mass Water in Arizona. We can produce enough food for all humanity. We need one reader to visualize it to realize it. Let's make dehydration and starvation available in only one place—a museum. As a bad memory and one never to be repeated.

Let's assume and believe that God is infinite. We are made in the image and likeness of God. Therefore we are infinite. In your unlimited reality, you are made of the stuff of the infinite. Therefore you've got infinite potential. Add your infinite potential to a definite purpose, visualize it completely, and repetitively play it in your mind's eye, then take massive action and voilà! You have results that have results. You are here to infinitely and positively impact the world.

Another affirmation: *I like money, and money likes me. It is fun to create infinite money, wealth, and riches. I love innovating profitable products, services, processes, and ideas. I have infinite money.*

When I started speaking and writing, I went bankrupt and financially upside down, so I commenced with less than zero. I started thinking right, visualizing right, talking right, and acting right in order to obtain infinite money, and you can too. There is infinite money circulating now. By visualizing want you want and how you will render the highest quantity and quality of service possible with a positive mental attitude, you will acquire it. Visualizing is the beginning of the process. It is a process that you will forever be using to acquire more and more for yourself and others.

Right now, say to yourself, *I have infinite money.*

If you start thinking that you're coming from infinite money, what shows up? Infinite money. But you can't see it if you've got blinders on. That's what we put on horses so they can't see what's around them. That's the prison we want to get out of. You get out of it with insight; then you find out that you are out of sight.

Get out of limited reality. One way to do this is to use music. When you're trying to do some serious visualizing and thinking, listen to great music, like Pachelbel's *Canon in D* or works by Steven Halpern or Yanni, especially when you're doing closed-eye processing.

Esteem is inside out. It's self-esteem, self-image, self-I-am-age, where you're going to talk yourself up, not down. We've all been taught excessively well how to talk ourselves down. I am encouraging you in the private room of your mind to visualize yourself up to extraordinary achievements and then to actively pursue them with vigor.

What was boxer Muhammad Ali's line? "I am the greatest." It made headlines when I was delivering the *Chicago Tribune* as a little nine year old kid; everyone said, "That guy's pretty arrogant, isn't he?" But he showed three times that he was the greatest. He was poetic in his psyching out his fighting foes by saying: "I dance like a butterfly. I sting like a bee. I am going to KO you in round three." That's declared visualization in action.

We've got to get out of addictive habits. That means changing the pictures in your mind. If you drink too much, smoke too much, eat too much, or sleep too much, that habit owns you. All you have to do is replace it with a better habit. As I learned from my friend Og Mandino, you can't get rid of a habit unless you give your mind a new, better habit that has more life force energy than the first one. You get rid of a lack of money by seeing yourself with lots of money. It's been one of my quests to get everyone out of poverty consciousness, because I grew up thinking that impoverishment was normal and natural.

You get rid of sickness by visualizing yourself as healthy. We've learned this from many doctors as well as the author Norman Cousins, who cured himself of a connective-tissue disease with laughter, and Dr. Bernie Siegel, author of *Love, Medicine, and Miracles*.

Visualizing is realizing, and you've got to decide to do it. When we're changing the models in our mind, we change the results in our lives. People don't choose something they can't believe in. None of us would try to establish colonies on the sun, because we don't believe that it would work.

Unfortunately, people don't have models for peace. We sing the song, "Let there be peace on earth, and let it begin with me," but say you go into the grocery store with somebody that you've watched sing that song, and their little kid is acting up. What do they do? They try to dislodge the kid's arm from his shoulder, shouting, "Will you listen to me?"

We all have lots of models of violence but very few models of peace. Who has to create those new models? We do.

A lot of us say, "It's not my fault. I was imprinted with these patterns from my parents, and I'm just doing what they did." That's not the program. You cannot fault your parents, because who's responsible for you, your behavior, and your actions?

You are.

My friend Wally Amos, founder of Famous Amos cookies, showed me the last four letters in *harmony—mony.* If you're in harmony, you also get all the money that you want. The trick is that you have to see it before you can have it.

I've been in poverty. After I went bankrupt, I had to sleep on a walk-in at the top of a staircase on the way into another guy's bedroom; he let me put a sleeping bag out in front of his room for six months. So I understand what it's like to be bummed out and feel you don't have the resources. I was so low that I had to reach up to touch bottom.

I had the resources available, but I didn't believe it, so I couldn't achieve it. I was so broke for a while that I came close to ripping off the milkman.

But then I saw myself in my idyllic environment. I said, "Someday I want to drive into my own estate in a luxury car. I want the gate to open up and then close behind me. I want to buzz down the window. I want the olfactory nature of my environment to imbue my nostrils and fluff up my aura. Why not own that place?"

In my house now, we have mock orange trees on the right. Behind us we've got night-blooming jasmine, whose fragrance wafts into the bedroom. We've got pine trees. We have ornamental and edible horticulture, like kumquats, around us. We even have an ornamental horticulturist who comes by to make sure that everything is growing and lovely.

We talk to the plants. We're in Southern California, so we have ever-blooming strawberries that produce fruit 365 days a year. My kids know how to grow and pick kumquats, as well as cherry tomatoes and everything else we grow. They know how to harvest avocados with a hook. That seems to me the kind of environment that you and I are meant to create, not an awful one.

Free Your Self-Esteem

Psychologists tell us that most of us only use 10 percent of our self-esteem. The deal is that when you free your self-esteem, you free yourself and others.

Right now, say, *I'm freeing my self-esteem and facilitating the freedom of others.*

Now pretend your hands are in bondage. Then say, *I'm breaking the bonds of my bondage, and I'm taking off the shackles and dropping them.* Feel yourself breaking the shackles off your wrists, and don't pick them up again.

We watch all this garbage on TV and the Internet. From the computer industry, we know garbage in equals garbage out. Therefore, if we put success in, what do we get out?

Success.

Who's the one that's in control of all of this?

Touch yourself and say, *Me.*

Say, *Being personally transformed, I leave behind fear.*

FEAR is an acronym. It means *false evidence appearing real.*

Leave behind guilt. You don't need it. Guilt always brings self-persecution, so there's no payoff and there's always a psychic whammy coming out of it.

Leave behind greed. How do you know if you are greedy? It comes down to just one question: am I a giving person? If you keep every one of the dollars you've got, then guess what? You're greedy. Mahatma Gandhi said: "There is enough for everyone's needs, but not everyone's greed."

You may say, "You don't understand, Mark. I'm already 110 percent overdrawn." I understand, and that's why you're 110 percent overdrawn—because you haven't been playing the system the way it's set up. The system says, "Give, and you shall receive."

If you don't have enough, then give whatever you've got. Give a smile, if that's all you got to give. Give a wink. Give reinforcing words. Give encouragement. Give a heartfelt letter of congratulations. You could almost congratulate everyone you talk to. They would inwardly figure out what you are congratulating them for and smile beamingly. Their reactions will surprise you.

Go into a convalescent home and go up to a guy who's had a stroke and has no use of half of his body. He is aphasic, meaning that his communications systems are no longer functioning. Just lean over and hug him. Every time I've watched friends do this when they were feeling beat-up, tears came out of their eyes. And the guy always grabs their hand and kisses it.

Life treats you the way you treat life. Al Sizer, my life insurance agent, and I are enormously close. Once he went to an extremely popular diner in Portland.

Al goes there for breakfast at 6:00 a.m., and there's already a line three blocks long. He thinks, "I haven't got time to wait a couple of hours. I don't like sitting at the counter, but I'll see if there's a counter seat."

There's one seat left. To Al's left is a lady who's wrapped in sixteen layers of clothes, taciturn, and shutdown, and who smells like mothballs. To his right is a tired-looking guy who is equally zipper-lipped.

Al thinks, "Maybe I can break through this guy a little more easily than this crotchety old lady." He does, and the guy starts to come unglued and effervesce. They have a wonderful time.

All of a sudden Al looks at his watch and said, "It's 9:30. I've got to split. It was nice meeting you. Here's my card. Give me one of yours."

The next Wednesday, the man comes to Al's office. Al's secretary hands him the man's card and says, "There's a guy sobbing out in the waiting room. He said you saved his life on Saturday."

Al says, "I don't do that. I don't know what you're talking about." He looks at the card and remembers the man. He tells his secretary, "Bring him in. I didn't plan on seeing him today, but bring him in."

The guy comes in, hugs Al, and says, "You saved my life on Saturday."

"I don't understand," says Al. "What do you mean I saved your life?"

"You couldn't have known it, but the day before, I went to the doctor; I was having stomach problems. He took X-rays, came back, and said that with my problems I'd be lucky if I lived a week. I couldn't face that kind of uncertainty. I decided to have the best meal I could, go up the highest building, jump off, and end it all. But because of your joy of living, I decided to live.

"Yesterday," the guy continues, "I went back to the doctor. He'd inadvertently switched the X-rays. He said there was nothing wrong except that I had an impacted descending colon, and we've taken care of it."

The point is that you don't know when a little thing like a smile will get you out of greed and into giving. The Dead Sea's only dead because it takes and it forgets to give. The principle is that living is giving, caring is sharing. Christ said the greatest person is one who serves the most.

When you meditate, ask, "What is it I can do to really serve colossally well? How can I not only serve colossally well, but lock it in and make it permanent?" The biggest question that Dr. Peter Diamandis, author of *Abundance*, cocreator of Singularity University, and creator of the XPRIZE, asks of everyone is: "What are you going to do to positively serve one billion people in the next decade?" That will get your visualizations into hyperoverdrive.

You give, and the giving keeps going after you're gone. Isn't that what Walt Disney did? Disney died in 1966, but his company has built places like Epcot, the Tokyo Disney Resort, the Shanghai Disneyland Park in China, even Disneyland Moscow.

That's the way to get out of scarcity and out of lack.

Right now, say, *I'm out of scarcity.*

I'm out of lack.

I'm in abundance.

I'm in plenty.

I'm in surplus.

And more surplus.

Go through your wardrobe. Take the stuff that doesn't fit, give it away to the Salvation Army, Goodwill, a church store, or a thrift store, and do it with love and gentility. Be grateful that it served you nicely and now will serve and benefit others. You will get new and better clothes in surprising and unexpected ways.

Transforming the World

Here's the principle: personal transformation precedes world transformation. The world transforms when we do. And as we transform, will we also transform the ecology?

I have a friend who was one of the big guys in the aerosol business. Once he and I were talking, and he said, "I can no longer do this business."

"Why not?" I said.

"I found out what aerosols are doing to the biosphere, and it's out of integrity for me or anyone else to do it, so I'm leaving the business."

He did. He got rid of that business and came away with $7 million in cash.

I asked him, "Do you know what you're going to do?"

"I'm going to rest for about six months."

"My dear friend, there's no way in God's little universe that you'll be able to take even one month off. I'll bet a grand that you can't do it." And in the end he paid.

My friend went to Russia—this was still in the Soviet era—on a peace mission. When he got there, he found that there were a lot of things that Russians didn't have, like copying machines, so he met with the executives there and ended up running their whole copier distribution and supply chain business.

We have to change the military-industrial complex. Bucky Fuller wrote a book entitled *Utopia or Oblivion*. When we get out of weaponry, we get into *livingry*. In fiscal 2019, the United States spent $686 billion on the military. If you ask any general whether that's enough to guarantee defense, they will all say no. Is $700 billion enough? No. Is $800 billion enough? No. Is $1 trillion enough? No. Then why keep spending it? Because that's the model.

Who has to change the model?

Say, *I do*.

You're probably familiar with Ken Keyes's book *The Hundredth Monkey*. It tells about an island off of Japan, where there were little monkeys that were eating dirty sweet potatoes. Some young monkeys started going down to the water to wash up their sweet potatoes. When a hundred of them, what we call *critical mass*, knew that you ought to have clean sweet potatoes, an interesting thing happened.

All the monkeys on that island started washing their sweet potatoes. Then anthropologists went to all the other nearby islands, and all the monkeys on them started washing their sweet potatoes at the same time, because it had reached critical mass.

Ken's book suggests that when we reach critical mass, we'll get out of weapons and into living. That can happen more than ever now, because we've got instant communications; thirty seconds after anything happens anywhere in the world, we know about it.

The teenage suicides in America break my heart, because these kids are coming out of such ignorance that they think they can go somewhere else when they die. As they watch their bodies fall away, they say, "Oh my God. I'm still here," because there's nowhere to go.

Individually, we can only shuffle off the physical container called our body. Our spirit is eternal. We live in a world where this is our full-time place to be, learn, grow, experience, and be consummate problem solvers—knowing that there is always a solution other than suicide. This is not a dress rehearsal. The young world needs to learn visualization and come to know that we live in the equivalent of a hologram. We create it visually from the inside out.

If life doesn't look like what you want, the only thing you get to do is remodel in your mind what you want it to look like. You are living in the reality of what you've been modeling. If you change the model, you change the result. It's just like a movie theater: if you put a different film in the projector, you'll get a different film to watch. Put in a different idea and you get a different out-picturing.

Next, we're going to change the economy. Bucky Fuller taught me that we've got to go to cosmic cost accounting. We're going to go to a brand-new accounting system, thanks to a plastic, fantastic reality. In the next twenty-five years, for the first time in history, it is possible that we're going to feed and house all of humanity. We're going to take care of everyone.

The transformation starts inside out. Right now, say, *I choose personal transformation and inspire others to do so too.*

Somebody may say, "That would be miraculous if it happened." If it'll happen for you, it could happen to others, because, "Each one, reach one. Each one, teach one." In the last century, Helen Kromer wrote this poem:

One man awake
Can waken another;
The second can waken
His next door brother.
The three awake
Can rouse a town,
By turning the whole
Place upside down.
The many awake
Can make such a fuss,
That it finally wakens
The rest of us!
One man up,
With dawn in his eyes,
Multiplies.

Who is it that's going to multiply? Say, *I am.*

Ideas are magnets. When you have an idea and you process it, you orbit around the idea, you get closer and closer to it, and you get better and better at it; pretty soon, when you have ownership of the idea, the idea takes ownership of you.

Rethinking the Olympics

When he was only fourteen, Peter Ueberroth decided that he would be financially free and independent. He wrote on a little goal card, "By the time I'm

thirty-five, I'll be financially free and independent."
I ask you to do the same thing. Write your goal on a
three-by-five card and carry it around wrapped in a
$100 bill. When you wrap your goals in a $100 bill,
the intent is to make you feel more prosperous, so
you become more prosperous.

Peter Ueberroth went on to build the second biggest travel agency in America and retired for exactly
one day. In 1984, Los Angeles got the Summer Olympics. The only other applicant for host city had been
Tehran, Iran, but that was withdrawn because of the
revolution there.

Los Angeles Mayor Tom Bradley said, "My God.
They lost $9 billion in the 1976 Olympics in Mon-
treal. We've got to get somebody to run them that's
a free enterpriser and a wise business person."

As an aside, my daddy taught my brothers and
me free enterprise. He said, "Free enterprise means
the more enterprising you are, the freer you are."
Nobody stops us from working more than a forty-
hour week. A forty-hour week is just a living. You've
got to put in fifty, sixty, seventy hours a week for
at least four or five years until you get to millionaire status. Generally, unless you have one colossally good idea that somebody else executes on your
behalf, you've got to put in your sweat equity and
mind equity first. And you're also building up your

own belief system. This means that you've got to earn all you can, save all you can, and invest all you can so you can be as philanthropic as you can and do the most good in the least amount of time with your money. It's sort of like becoming an Olympian. It takes herculean efforts at the front end to become financially strong and independent.

Anyhow, Bradley goes to Ueberroth, says, "Look, we've got the Olympics. I want you to run it, because they lost $9 billion in Montreal."

"I'd love to," Ueberroth said. "I'll take the challenge. What will you pay me?"

"A dollar a year," said Bradley.

Then Ueberroth asks, "How much have you got to underwrite the Olympics?"

"Nada, because we didn't plan on it. We don't have anything."

Ueberroth understood that ideas are magnets: they bring you the people, the resources, the time, the talent, the skills, the energy, and other complementary ideas. The minute you have an idea of what to do, your subconscious visually figures out *how*. Romans 11:33 says that God's ways "are past finding out." You've got to know *what you want*; the subconscious figures out *how to make it happen*.

Ueberroth, going into deep meditation, asked, "How am I going to make the Olympics work? What do I need to do to get the money?" He decided to get private funding.

Ueberroth also said, "Every Olympics has had buildings that have never been used again, so I'm going to build buildings that get reused, and we're not going to pay for them." Ueberroth got Coca-Cola to bid against Pepsi, and Kodak to bid against Fiji Film. He did that with every industry and got fully privately funded. He did it because he visualized the end from the beginnings and exceeded with excellence.

In the end, Ueberroth got 7-Eleven to fund the Olympic Velodrome, while McDonald's paid for the Olympic Swim Stadium. The Los Angeles Olympics were a financial success, securing twice the amount of income (adjusted for inflation) received by the 1980 Moscow Olympics and four times that of the 1976 Montreal Olympics.

Three

Sourcing the Subconscious

As I wrote in my *Future Diary*, you ought to have a list of two hundred people you want to meet and spend time with, grow with and be expanded by. Write down who they are specifically, and then write down the questions you want to ask them. It also behooves you to go online, get their picture, and put it next to yours. That simple act gets your mind believing it will happen, and voilà! It will.

This happened to me years ago. I'm standing in line at a rent-a-car place in Hawaii. The guy next to me sneezes. Just out of courtesy, I say, "Gesundheit." He spins around. He turns out to be the head of economic development in Hawaii, and he'd sat in on several of my seminars. He said, "Hi, Mark."

"Delighted to see you again," I said.

Now one of the people that I wanted to meet was Chris Hemmeter. He built the ultimate destination resorts in Hawaii, and at the time he was building one on the Big Island of Hawaii: the Hyatt Regency Waikoloa (today the Hilton Waikoloa Village). I wanted to go to the grand opening.

Hemmeter was a guy who started with nothing, but he wanted to be a builder in Oahu. He goes to Cornell, comes back, and builds a fantastic hotel, the Hyatt Regency Waikiki. He makes no money on the rooms, but makes a lot of money on the concessions. A lot of people have the idea that they've got to make money in what they're mainlining, but sometimes you've got to make money on the peripherals, on the surplus or what we call in the speaking business the backend.

In any case, I wanted to meet Hemmeter, and this guy's standing next to me. I say, "Isn't he opening up the ultimate resort here in Waikoloa?"

"Soon," he says, "As a matter of fact, Friday, September 2. I have two tickets, and my wife doesn't want to go."

"Is that an invitation?"

"Do you want it to be?"

"I want it to be."

So my wife and I went. I was there when they dropped a quarter million orchids on us. Hemmeter made it totally Disneyesque. You entered by a gondola and passed by millions of dollars' worth of Asian-American art, or you went in on a monorail and passed nineteen restaurants. This guy had 31,000 acres to play on, including the biggest man-made lagoon in the world, which had eight dolphins. The next day I went there with my wife, my two kids, and my housekeeper, and we got to play and swim with the dolphins, taking endless pictures while creating cherishable memories.

The point is, if you put whom you want to meet in writing and in pictures that are emotionally impregnated into your mind, magically those people shows up. Chris Hemmeter created the whole concept of the destination resort. Why? Because he had the idea that he could pull it off. He did, and everybody benefits. He had the idea of thinking big.

Hemmeter was also a great networker. When Jimmy Carter was president, Hemmeter had him stay his house, then he went to create, design, and invent the $25 million Jimmy Carter Museum in Georgia. When Ronald Reagan was president and

Yasuhiro Nakasone was prime minister of Japan, they both met at Hemmeter's house in Hawaii, and the next day he sold the Hyatt Oahu to the Japanese.

When you're visualizing, understand that your mind does best when it is multitasking. Isn't that a great term? When you task computers linearly, they work linearly. When you multitask in your mind—meaning that you keep adding assignments—they grow geometrically and can succeed exponentially. That's why I say when you set goals, set too many goals—at least, 101 goals that you want and believe you can achieve.

When we're visualizing, there's a danger of thinking, "If this were such a good idea, somebody else would have done it already."

No. There's only one doer in your universe. Who's that? You.

When you decide to do it, all the other powers come. You have lots of power, and the more you do, the more you can do.

Dr. Abe Maslow, the father of modern self-image psychology, says, "Quantity changes first, then quality improves." What does that mean? It means you've got to have fundamental happiness. You've got to get up a little bit in Maslow's hierarchy of needs, as it were. You have to take care of your physicality. You've got to be well before you can go forward.

You've got to be out of hunger before you can go on to the next level.

Now I'm also going to give you the contrary philosophy of thinking small, because it works too. When the Japanese came here with their cars in the 1960s, the United States had almost 100 percent of the automobile market. Anything that came from Japan was called junk.

What did the Japanese do? They kept doing what is called the "matrix of squares," which is brilliant. It's based on the principle of how can I improve and do it better?

The Japanese kept putting the matrix over smaller and smaller elements to make their cars better. Eventually they had the best cars, and now they have around 40 percent of the American automobile market.

How do you use this principle in your own life? You say, "As good as my relationships are with my family, how do I improve them and make them better? As good as my relationships are with those who I work with, how do I make them better? As good as my relationships are at home, how do I make them more harmonious? How do I make them more ordered, more wondrous?" Then, "How do I go from my own visualization to making the world work?"

Inspirational thinker Emmet Fox says, "If you want peace in the world, it starts with you and goes out." When you meditate, wrap yourself in white light. First of all, you put white light around yourself. Then you put it around your family, then around your house, then around the state, then around the country, and then you send it into the capitals around the world. Then you have the radius go around the whole planet to empower it and make it secure.

Why not do that? If you do it before something happens, then you're even safer, you're even better off.

If You Had Everything

If you were provided with absolutely everything you need and wanted to release your full potential and your highest vision on behalf of yourself and humanity, what would you do? Read this aloud.

If I were provided with absolutely everything I want and need to release my full potential, to release my highest vision for myself and humanity, and I knew that all the resources and people, talent, time, tools, technology, and finance were there for me, what would I do for myself? What would I do for myself and what would I do for all of humanity?

Close your eyes and meditate on this. When you hit upon an answer, open your eyes and jot it down.

Even if you don't get the answer instantly, you will have it imminently; it may come in the middle of the night.

Tonight, when you go to bed, make sure you have next to your bed paper and pencil or pen, or a recording device, such as the one on your smartphone. You may have had great ideas in the middle of the night and said, "Oh, boy. That's great. I'll remember it in the morning," but did you?

One person I wanted to meet was comedian Red Skelton, and I did. We met in the United Airlines private lounge at Los Angeles International Airport. I said, "Red, I have been a fan of yours for a long time." He jokingly said, "It's a hot day; I need a fan."

I said, "Is it true that you've got a photographic memory?" He said, "Yeah; it's not developed yet."

He told me this story. "The other night I was meditating, and all of a sudden, I came up with the idea for the greatest show that has ever been written." So Red said, "'I'm going to write this thing down,' and I did. I woke up the next morning, and I knew it was going to be perfect. I looked at what I'd written, and it said, 'Write play.' I couldn't remember a thing."

When you have an idea, you've got to write it down instantly. The more you write your ideas down, the more your subconscious will feed them to you and tell you how to manifest them. The more you go with your feeling, your intuition, your gut, the more will come. The more you use your subconscious, source it, and take notes on it, the more it will feed forward—faster, better, higher, and more wonderful.

Meeting Lou Tice

I've got an example about this point that I want to share with you.

I did a tour of Australia—a great, wonderful country, a continent in its own right, with has a tiny population (26 million people) and very few in the interior; they basically only live in coastal regions. Eventually we arrived in Perth, in Western Australia. Perth and West Perth are where just about everybody lives in this giant state. Western Australia is to Australia what California is to America. It's the thinking, innovative, and tech mecca. It's probably got more millionaires than any other place in Australia.

Anyhow, I was doing an early morning breakfast talk for the National Speakers Association there. A man said, "One of your mates is here from America, your colleague in this business of speaking."

"Who's that?"

"Lou Tice is speaking after lunch."

"I've always wanted to hear him. See if you can score me a ticket."

The guy said, "I don't think that will be a problem. I'll call you back by 10:00."

The guy called back at 10:00 and said, "I'm really sorry, but the tickets are sold out; it's standing room only."

A little incensed, I went into meditation. I figured that if you're meant to be there, there's a ticket. I asked, "Why am I being denied entry into seeing Tice?" My subconscious said, "There's only one flight every day out of Perth to Melbourne, and he and his wife are going to be on it tomorrow morning. Don't let your good get in the way of your better."

Next morning, sure enough, I get on a plane with Earl Nightingale, the cofounder and main voice at that time of the Nightingale-Conant Company in Chicago. Three seats ahead of us also in first class are Lou Tice and his wife, Diane.

"There are the Tices," I say to Earl.

"Who's he?"

"Earl, he's about three times as big as you are in our business."

"Then why don't I know about him?"

"I think you've read everything, but you've missed some of the stuff in our own business."

Earl says, "I want to meet him when we get off the plane."

"Why wait? We've got six hours of encapsulated space."

So Earl asks Lou if we could meet with him.

We spent six hours enraptured. Even though we were in the flight attendants' way, we just reveled in thinking and talking outloud and sharing ideas of how to work together profitably. If you want to make a long flight go fast, get with somebody who knows the art of conversation, who is living on the leading edge of conversation and reality, who is excited, who is doing things that nobody else has ever done before, who wakes up levels of your imagination, so that like an onion, you keep pulling back layer after layer.

Sitting with the Tices, we had the time of our life. We didn't finish our conversation. Even though we had six hours, if you're with somebody that is tuned in, six hours is only the front end. If most of the professors in most universities in America were to talk nonstop for six hours, you'd exhaust their bank of information. When you're with somebody who understands that life starts with the idea and it keeps generating, six hours is not enough.

Lou said, "We've got to get together again. Would you have any time to stop by our place? Our headquarters, the Pacific Institute, is in Seattle, Washington."

"I'm coming out of Vancouver next week," I said. "I'd love to."

When I get there, he has his whole board of directors ready to grill me. A guy sitting to my left has the most gruesome face I've ever seen. As Emerson said, "Who you are speaks so loudly that I can't hear what you're saying." Your countenance is who you are. That's why old Abe Lincoln said, "Up to age forty, you control the lines in your face. After that, they control you." If you ever see people who go around harrumphing, they look that way on the outside because they're harrumphing on the inside.

Later, at lunch, I say to Lou, "Lou, tell me about the guy who was to my left. He has a gruesome countenance. What is the deal?"

"He's the first guy you've ever met that stabbed to death nineteen people in Brooklyn, New York, and has a 246-year prison sentence. He's been paroled to the Tices to be rehabilitated."

"What kind of company are you running?" I said.

"Mark," he said, "wouldn't it be a miracle if we take prisoners, get them out of prison, and keep them out of prison permanently? Using the stuff that I'm about, we're sharing my videos; we're getting people out of prison and keeping them out. The penal system, as we've got it, isn't working. We don't even have enough room for them.

"Look," he went on, "we work with what we call chronic welfare victims. A welfare victim has just got the wrong image in their head. They have the image that 'I'm a victim. Oh, poor me. Isn't it awful? I'm a victim.' They may have come through several generations of that.

"We change the pictures in their mind," Lou goes on. "We get them off welfare. We work with them for free for two years, at the end of which, if they're still off welfare—and 98 percent of them are—we get paid by $100,000 a person by the U.S. government." It costs $1.8 million to keep them on welfare. Isn't it cheaper to use his program?

What's the principle here? Change the vision, and you change the result. The scriptures say: "Without vision, the people perish" (Proverbs 29:18). To translate positively, I say with vision we can flourish, shine, and rise to unexpected heights. And you can perish while you're still physically here. Some people are born in 1960, died in 1985, but didn't get buried till 2010. They're dead in mind. They are brain-damaged and brain-dead.

"What else are you doing?" I said.

He had thirty-one major programs. "Look," he said, "I'm just a high-school coach that decided to make a difference."

Right now, say *I'm making a difference.*

You start where you are, whether you're ready or not. So say, *I'm starting whether I'm ready or not.*

At one point Lou was going to Ireland. He said, "I think I can help change the pictures in those people's minds, so they don't have religious strife there." Harmony is inside out. People can get along and have harmony even if they've been fighting for four hundred years over nothing.

All religions started at the same place. If we only had one start for humanity, whether it was two people or ten, we all started the same. We've all got the same roots. It makes sense now that for the first time with interconnected communication, transportation, and computerization, we're going to get along all over again.

Then I asked Lou, "What are you doing after that?"

"I'm going into South Africa." This was before the end of apartheid. "I'm also going into Pakistan and India."

Lou Tice was coming up with a new model. He said, "I'd recommend, Mark, that you encourage yourself and others to look at problems in a new way."

You're Bigger than the Problem

If you stay at the level of the problem, you don't solve it. It's over; you can't do anything. Bucky Fuller said, "The goal is to go inside your mind, transcend the problem, and look down on it."

You're bigger than the problem. Whatever your problem is, there's somebody in the world that could solve it. Take their mantle, take their mind power, and put it on you.

Pretend there's a mantle in front of you. Put it on and say, *I'm putting on a new mental mantle. I can solve those problems.*

Billionaire H. Ross Perot was constantly coming up with new ideas. In the 1980s, he bought 16,300 acres outside of Dallas airport. Now most people would say, "My God, you shouldn't compete with Dallas Fort Worth Airport."

At the time, oil prices were low, and people in Texas were also saying, "We're going to be broke and stay broke."

Perot said, "You're not broke because of the oil business. High oil prices benefit the few, not the many. As far as I'm concerned, I'm for lower oil prices and getting us off the oil business. I'm going to employ more people in Dallas than anyone ever has before. I'll get Dallas back working, and I'm doing it just for one reason—to show you there's no reason to have lack thoughts and base your thinking on one product."

Everybody said, "What if it doesn't work?"

"It doesn't matter," he said. "I've got deep pockets. It was my idea. I'm backing my idea."

Most people go to you and say, "Back my idea." But the first person who has to back your idea is you.

So Perot built Fort Worth Alliance Airport, which opened in 1988. It's the second largest airport in Texas, just behind Dallas Fort Worth.

Switzerland is another example. They have very few resources. What did they do? They decide to make money—banking—a resource, and that has been a pretty rich source of income. Then they said, "We could make the best watches, and we could ship them to everybody and charge a fortune." Switzerland also chose to be one of the chocolate making capitals of the world.

The danger is that you might get stuck. Bucky Fuller said, "You are not born with roots." You may have been born with roots, but metaphorically and metaphysically, you are bipedal. You can walk around. You can move. You are not rooted. He wrote another great book about this principle called *I Seem to Be a Verb*.

Our job is to empower the empowerers, to put the whole program together and see it grow bigger, better, more wondrous, more magnificent, and more fulfilling for self and for all of humanity. We need visionary leaders that lead.

We get many letters from people that say, "Until you showed me a new picture, I didn't know that I could source and serve total humanity."

Lou Tice said, "Here's the basic picture that all of us come out of. We come out of restrictive motivation: I have to go to work on Monday. I have to carry out the garbage." If you have to carry out the garbage, then do it with love, do it with dignity, do it with affection. Make sure it's wrapped in plastic so you don't smell it and it won't get on you.

If you earn enough money, you hire somebody else to carry out the garbage. I don't like doing it; it is not the highest and best that I can be, so I've hired the kid next door to do it. He doesn't know how to turn money as I do, so it's good for him. He thinks it's wonderful. He's only getting $10, because he hasn't been using his head right. I invite him to the seminars, but he hasn't come; it's his tough luck. I said, "I can make you a millionaire before you're twenty if you just learn the principles, because principles work whether you're male or female, tall or short."

I wrote a book called *The Richest Kids in America*. I interviewed twenty-one kids who, using their individual self-initiative to action, earned over a million dollars before turning nineteen years old. They are inspirationally amazing and a joy to work with at my seminars and meetings. They've gotten many other youngsters that read, watched, or heard them to think their way out of lack and into lots of money. They have made so much that many of them hired their parents, teachers, and friends to work for them.

Steve Jobs and Steve Wozniak were mastermind partners. They built the first personal computer in a garage and just went forward. One of the places they looked at for technology was the Xerox Corporation. Xerox had developed the mouse, they had developed Windows, but they weren't using these technologies. Why? They had the wrong picture. They were in restrictive motivation: "We can't afford it. We're on an austerity program." Note: Austerity programs always and only create lack and limitation and thwart initiatives governmentally, corporately, and personally.

While Xerox were thinking and experiencing deprivation and what they couldn't be, do or have, Apple said, "Wow! We can vastly and profitably improve computing with this one innovation," which became worth billions. Xerox lost billions with erroneous thinking and Steve Jobs made billions by visualizing a solution and then solving the problem.

In the 1970s, New York City was on an austerity program and was on the verge of going bankrupt. It was the consensual consciousness of the people in the city and of Abe Beame, who was mayor at the time. As far as I'm concerned, he was off the beam. He kept saying, "New York's going bankrupt."

What did businesses do? It was self-fulfilling prophecy they left New York City, just as they did during the 2020 pandemic. What you see is what you get.

In 1977, a new mayor, Ed Koch, comes in. He says, "New York's doing wonderfully. It's booming." All the businesses came back. The city came out of restrictive motivation into constructive motivation.

Right now, say, *I'm into constructively being motivated.*

Notice the word I put in there: *being.* My friend Og Mandino says you're not a human being, you're a human becoming. The change here is critical. When you are in a state of lack, you are, metaphorically speaking, a caterpillar. You are probably in a cocoon state now; you're feeling inspirational discontent and you want to punch out of that thing.

Today's your day to punch out. Right now, say, *I'm punching out, and I'm becoming a butterfly.* Break out of the cocoon. Plan to go into high flight of success and achievement. Punch out with your hand.

The more you do this, the more you're in a state of mind of "I do it because I want to." America came out of the cocoon of the 1890s depression with four money generating inventions that made our industrial revolution because of the visions of these men: Alexander Graham Bell created the telephone. The Wright Brothers flew at Kitty Hawk and started aviation. Edison created electricity and lit the world. Henry Ford developed the assembly line for mass-producing automobiles. Today we are about to exit the cocoon into the greatest boom in business ever, with technology and innovation leading the way to a $50 trillion dollar economy, I predict, between 2020 and 2030.

Why not make a Garden of Eden out of your whole life and world? Why not decide to have fresh flowers on your desk every day? Why not have your office and home smell fresh and alive, green with plants, healthy and good? Why not have botanicals all the way around your house and office, giving off negative ions, which are life force energy? Why not go walking on the beach every morning? Why not decide to take in all that life has and see all the places there are to see in the world? If you think about it enough, you can get other people to pay for it. I travel first-class around the world, and my clients are delighted to pay for my wife and me to work with them. So far we have been to eighty countries and talked to and inspired over seven million people. At seventy-two years young, I feel I am just beginning.

Recently I was in Charleston and got an insider tour. I saw where the Civil War started, with the shelling of Fort Sumter. I saw the awful pain of America, because that's where all the slaves came in. I'm sorry that we had that blemish in our history, but I'm glad that we had people like President Abe Lincoln to eliminate slavery with the Emancipation Proclamation.

Get out of restrictive motivation, get back into constructive motivation, and break through. All it takes to have all of us break through is for one of us to break through.

Who's that one?

Say, *I am*.

Now understand you've just made a viable, vital, valuable stand by saying that you're the one. *I am* is God's name in nature and the universe. Whatever you add to those words *I am* you become instantly and constantly. The danger is, you've just bought into a bigger reality, and whether you want it or not, all of the universe is rushing in to say yes.

Armand Hammer's Journey

Let me give an example—the late financier Dr. Armand Hammer. He's one of my heroes. At one point, Hammer was going to the Columbia University medical school, doing really well. His father, Julius, a medical doctor who came out of Russia, was a socialist at the wrong time. Tammany Hall didn't like it. He performed an abortion, and the lady died. They put him in the slammer. Julius called his son to jail and said, "I'm going to be here for a while. They don't like me. They've essentially thrown away the key. Figure out, Armand, how to get me out of here. We own one of the biggest pharmacies here in the Battery in New York. Please make it work."

Hammer got a guy to be his roommate in Greenwich Village, and he let him live there free. This guy took notes at medical school at night. He'd come home, bring the notes, and read them to Armand. Armand studied them. He never went to class again for the last two years of medical school, but ended up graduating cum laude. I respect that, because I graduated high school cum lousy.

This is a critical point, because it doesn't matter what you *haven't* been. IQ is irrelevant; it measures where you've been, not where you can go if you've got a magnificent obsession. As Lee Iacocca, the late

CEO of Chrysler, said, "When you light the match and you get on fire, watch out, because your IQ goes straight up." I may have been a dolt earlier, but I'm not anymore, and I'm going on to higher ground—just as you can. Say, *I can too.* Your *I can* is vastly more important and influential than your IQ.

You've got to get rid of negative inner messages—"I don't remember things" or "I'm forgetful" or "I'm a Calamity Jim or Jane." All that stuff is idiocy and low-mindedness, and it comes out of yesterday. In my tomorrows, I know it all.

Say, *In my tomorrows, I know it all. In my today, I know it all.*

In any case, Hammer goes into the father's pharmacy and he finds out what they're selling profitably—tincture of ginger. He doesn't know why that's working. He finds out who's buying it, goes down to Virginia to see them, and learns they use tincture of ginger to spike and make bootleg whiskey; it's during Prohibition.

Hammer corners the market for tincture of ginger and makes $2 million in a few days. He sells out his whole company back to the workers through an employee stock ownership plan: an ESOP.

Hammer graduates from medical school and reads in the paper that in his parents' homeland, Russia, people are suffering bubonic plague. He gets a $100,000 medical wagon together and takes it at his own expense to Russia. When he arrives, he sees that people aren't suffering from bubonic plague; they are starving. The news story that he read was face-saving communist propaganda. Armand calls his brother Victor, who's been his partner through life, and says, "Buy some food and ship it over here as fast as you can." He starts feeding people immediately.

When you're thinking and visualizing new models, are you going to get a lot of attention? Yes. If you don't want it or can't handle it, let somebody else be the face person, because you're also going to get lots of critics.

Hammer meets with the Soviet leader, Lenin, who says, "Doctor Hammer, we don't need doctors. We need good businessmen, and we need to feed Russia. You're a millionaire; buy a million dollars' worth of food. Bring it here, and I'll give you business concessions to bring caviar and fur back to the United States. We also need you to work with Henry Ford and buy our farmers tractors."

Now if you know anything about Henry Ford, you know he was anticommunist. Armand, now a twenty-three-year-old doctor, comes in to see Henry Ford. Ford says, "Get out of here, you Bolshevik commie pinko sympathizer."

Like Columbo in the old TV show, Hammer is about to leave but turns around and says, "One more question, Mr. Ford, before I exit gracefully."

"What's that?" said Ford.

"I understand you've been having trouble selling tractors," he says; "nobody's buying them." (This illustrates a major point: Always get your deep and comprehensive information first.) "You've been having trouble selling tractors. I've got a $1 million check in my pocket for Ford tractors."

"Young man, come back and sit down," says Ford.

If you haven't read Hammer's biography, *Hammer*, read it, because it reads better than a Sidney Sheldon novel. The guy's got a problem on every page, but he takes every one and turns it into an opportunity. You can't have a problem without having a bigger opportunity come along with it.

The yin and yang symbol is six thousand years old, and it means, "Crisis equals opportunity." Today we are having the biggest crisis ever worldwide; therefore with visualization we can invent the biggest opportunities ever.

I define and entrepreneur as someone who finds a problem and fixes it for a vast, fast profit. Everyone can become an entrepreneur. As I write this, thanks to the coronavirus lockdown, America has 30 million unemployed people, which is, from the right point of view, the biggest opportunity ever. Take my definition of entrepreneurship and profitably exploit it. Every adversity has a golden opportunity inside it waiting for you to discover and profit from it.

Watch Out for Labels

Another example is John Johnson, a black gentleman who gets a scholarship to go to University of Chicago but can't afford room and board. So he interviews for a job at Supreme Life Insurance Company, which sells to black people.

Johnson says, "I can't go to school, because I can't afford it." The head of the company says, "You work here, and we'll make sure you get through school. I'll make sure you get enough time to work."

Johnson does direct mail for Supreme. Then one day he reads *Reader's Digest* and realizes that black people need their own version of that magazine. He goes to the head of Supreme and says, "You've got twenty thousand policyholders. Let me do a direct mail piece to all those people, because that's what I do for you anyhow, and see if they would buy *Negro Digest*," which today is called *Ebony* magazine.

Johnson sends out twenty thousand pieces of mail, gets three thousand orders at $2 an order, and his magazine is born. Eventually Johnson became the first black American to make the Forbes 400. He said, "Nobody would buy any stock in my company when I began, and I'm not letting any of them have any now."

Johnson said, "I'm changing the image of black people by giving them new models and showing them images of success." It's not just black people that need those images. White people need them, kids need them—everybody needs them.

When you're breaking out of the old model and getting into the new one, beware of labeling. Labeling is dangerous. As the great Danish philosopher Søren Kierkegaard said, "Labeling always understates who we can become."

I live near a kid who's told that he's handicapped by the world, by society, by our school system. But he's not. This guy does a whole Snoopy exhibition on his front lawn. Every year this guy makes a new major model of Snoopy, Linus, and other *Peanuts* characters. Even though society calls him handicapped, these models are as good as anything you could see at Disneyland. This guy may be handicapped in reading; he may have dyslexia—which is now curable—he may have all kinds of things going against him, but the societal label is wrong, because this guy is giving all he knows how to give with these magnificent, bigger than life-sized models. The creator of Snoopy and Charlie Brown, Charles

"Sparky" Schulz, visualized cartoons that celebrate rejected losers, who are in pain and hurting. Charles heard about my young neighbor and came to see him with media in tow. It made this young man's efforts pay off with joy, love, and unforgettable excitement—memories that he will cherish forever. It also brought out many more visitors.

Four

Have a Vision

Somebody may ask, "Is it really that important to have a vision?" Yes. Once I was talking at a church in Santa Cruz, California. Afterward a lady came up to me; she was trembling, and she had bloodshot eyes and tears coming down her cheeks. She said, "Last night my son tried to kill himself. He's going to school here, and he's a straight-A student in two subjects—business and German. He tried to slash his wrists. His father feels so hurt that he wouldn't even come and see his own son. I haven't had the courage to go myself. I found out you're talking here. Would you go and see my boy with me?"

I don't particularly want to go see some kid who's just tried to cancel out his life, but his mother is very much in need, and I figure I could help her. I go over with her to see the kid in a mental institution.

They have the kid in a locked room. I go in and I ask him, "What do you really want?"

"I'm fluent in German," he said. "I've been getting straight A's in business and in German. After I graduate here, I want to go to Germany and work in a German company, but everybody says it's not possible. I've invested four years in studying sixteen hours a day, seven days a week. To hell with them. I'm killing myself. It's over."

I said, "That's all you want—to work in a German company? I can arrange that."

"How can you do that?"

"I was a student ambassador, and I'm pretty well-connected. I just did a talk for the organization that takes American students and places them in foreign countries. We take German students and place them in IBM. I'm well-connected, and as soon as you get out of here, I'll get you an assignment over there."

"If I'd met you a day before," he said, "I wouldn't have tried to commit suicide."

The point is that you and I can empower a lot of other people. If everyone else says, "You can't," you've got to find a way that says, "I can." There are infinite opportunities. We live in an infinite universe, where the only power that exists is mind power.

As comedian Flip Wilson's character Geraldine used to say, "What you see is what you get." The question is, what do you see inside the theater of your mind? It doesn't matter what you have; it matters where you're going. Spiritually, it's not who you are, but *whose* you are. You are a child of God Almighty, and He doesn't make any junk. We all need positive mentors who can tell us how to do what we want to do instead of parents, teachers, preachers, or advisors who say that you have wasted your life and you can't do this or that. You make your own decision. As Ralph Waldo Emerson said, "Be self-reliant! Spread joy and sunshine!"

Evergreen Opportunities

Once I did a talk in Portland, Oregon. A man came up to me afterward and said, "You're hired."

"Thank you very much," I said, "but I'm not looking for work with your company."

"No, no, I want you to speak six times in one day in my little home city of McMinnville, Oregon."

"That's a great amount of work in one day."

"You're up to it. Have you ever done that many in one day?"

I said no. But Bob Hope did that many, and he was the greatest human philanthropic institution in America, so I thought I would give it a shot.

In between times, I went back to this man's office. His name was Del Smith, and he owned Evergreen Airlines.

"How did you start?" I asked him.

"At seven years old, I was orphaned. Grandma Smith taught me, and she gave me all these great maxims—what you call affirmations. She said, 'We can have quality without compromise. We believe in work ethic and work opportunity in this family, Delford. I want you to read Napoleon Hill's *Think and Grow Rich.*' I got into her energy orbit, and she mesmerized me. She really made me believe that I should work. She didn't tell me what to do; she just told me to figure out what I want to do and do it. When I was nine years old, I went down to a bank in McMinnville, and I borrowed $2.50 to buy a lawnmower. I didn't know any better, so I went across the street and I borrowed $2.50 more from another bank for the same lawnmower. Back in the thirties, I was cutting lawns at 15 cents each. Some of them were as big as golf courses.

"By the time I was eleven years old—that was 1941—I'd saved $100, which was an awesome amount for me. Grandma Smith took such good care of me that I bought her a house for $100 down, with thirty-year financing, at 2 percent interest. Back in 1941, you could do that in McMinnville.

"When it was time to go to college, I didn't have enough money, but Grandma Smith's house had been appreciating in value, and I said, 'Can we borrow money out of the house so I could go to school?'

"She said, 'Del, I'd love you to. You bought it.'

"I'm in school. I'm doing all right," he went on. "I was reading *Life* magazine and saw that Igor Sikorsky had invented the helicopter. Mark, you say there's all the power in the world in the idea. I don't know what it was, but I caught Sikorsky's vision.

"I saw myself flying those helicopters. I graduated as fast as I could and enlisted in the United States Air Force. I was going to be in the helicopter service, but they tested me, found out I was color-blind and said, 'We're sorry, Del, but you can't fly.'

"That's OK, I thought. When I get out of here— I've been an entrepreneur since I was a little kid— I'll buy my own helicopter. At age twenty-five, I did, and I've never looked back. I just kept going forward, and I built this thing called Evergreen Airlines."

"Mark," he went on, "there's one thing that kids can't do."

"What's that?"

"They can no longer borrow money from a bank."

"Well, Del, why don't we start a kid's bank?"

I went for a little tour and the helicopter operation came back an hour later. Donna Nelson, senior vice president of the company, said, "Good news."

"What's that?" I asked.

"Del just started the Mark Victor Hansen's Children's Free Enterprise Bank."

"No kidding."

She told me that he had funded it with $25,000.

I said, "I didn't promise matching funds, did I? If I did, my wife will kill me."

The next day the Oregon banking commissioner closed down the bank, as he should have, because kids cannot sign contracts for money. We would have had all kinds of problems.

I'm sitting in Del's office. He calls up his law firm and says, "Do you guys like to get paid?"

"We do," they say.

"Then figure out a way to make Mark's bank work."

So the name was changed to the Children's Free Enterprise Fund. We don't lend children money; we grant it to them. They pay it back with interest. They've got to come into the bank building to learn the process. So far all the kids that have ever borrowed money from us have paid it back.

They've done wondrous things. A little girl, a sixth-grader, wanted to publish her little inspirational book. She sold six hundred copies in the first month and paid back the loan with interest. A kid in 4-H wanted to have a rabbit farm; he started it, and it's still prospering.

We had a kid who wanted to go to college but had absolutely no resources. His parents were stone broke; they'd always been living trying to rub two nickels together. Dan Corrigan, the chairman of the fund, said, "Look, I made a lot of money going to college washing windows; would you let me show you how?"

The kid said, "I don't have the money even to buy the basic resources or get a sign printed."

Dan said, "The bank will lend you $250. No problem."

We started that program. We've got lots of kids doing paper routes. I did not know that blind people could not work without a seeing-eye dog. We've lent a lot to blind kids so they could get seeing-eye dogs and work. It's just amazing. Every one of the kids pays it back. We're going to make it a worldwide event.

As good as the idea is, we want to make it better. Free enterprise is one of the things that make America great, which is why we have no emigration quotient; we only have immigration quotients.

My housekeeper saw herself coming to America, the land of opportunity. She watched her twin sister fall headfirst 400 feet onto the rocks while trying to cross the border. We've helped her get amnesty and full legality; she is a great, productive human being who has come to America. I worked with her to become a full citizen and attended her tear-generating graduation.

My dad came here from Denmark because this was the land of opportunity and the home of the brave. He could see it, even though he didn't have it. He was brave to come with no language skills, friends, or connections. He worked hard, and eventually, with the great work ethic he instilled in me, he owned Elite Bakery in Waukegan, Illinois, on the main business street in town. I am proud my dad exemplified the courage and conviction to go and become an American, because he would loudly say "I hate socialism, communism, and totalitarianism." I agree. Those isms are tested, tried, and terrible. Only free-enterprise capitalism works, thanks to our Founding Fathers, who wrote these principles into law and order.

See It First

You've got to see it before you can have it. That's what visualization is about. The beauty of visualization is that it can take you from poverty to prosperity; it can take you from sickness to total health. If you are not sick, it does not necessarily mean you're into high-level wellness. Why not decide to nurture every atom of your being all the way through? I'm going to live to be 127 years old, with options for renewal.

Comedian George Burns said he would live to the age of a hundred. "How can you live to be a hundred?" people asked.

"I can live to be a hundred if I am booked," he said. "I'm booked at the Palladium on my hundredth birthday. I'm a Jewish gentleman. They've paid me in advance. I can't afford to die."

And in fact he died about six weeks after his hundredth birthday.

Burns had an amazingly loving relationship with his late wife, Gracie Allen. After twenty-four years, he still went to see her once a month; he would bring her flowers and talk to her. As far as he was concerned, she was still alive. It doesn't matter where you are; the people in your life and can stay alive in your imagination.

In Steven Spielberg's classic film *E.T., the Extra-Terrestrial*, E.T. is leaving his friend Elliott. Elliott says, "You won't be here." E.T. points to Elliott's third eye between his eyebrows (for those of you that know about such things) and says, "I'm always in there." He hugs him and says goodbye. The point is that your whole life is in your mind. The only person you ever get to meet is in your imagination.

Tom Sullivan is a man for whom I have the highest admiration. As a child, he inadvertently lost his sight because of a mishap at the hospital, but he never blamed other people.

Given current technology, we cannot make him sighted again, but he's never let himself be less than a fully functioning individual. He has a movie that I would recommend. It's positive; it's uplifting. It's called *If You Could See What I Hear*. He also has a book out with the same title; if you read it, it will touch you. Here's a guy who is a fully functioning human being and has never let anything slow him down.

In 1968, Tom was wrestling for the United States of America with a Russian and was three seconds from getting pinned. He thought, "I can't lose. I don't want to dishonor America." He popped out one of his glass eyes and said, "Oh, my God. I lost an eye." The Russian could speak English, so he could understand him; he got up and started to vomit. Tom won.

One of my friends in Detroit hired Tom. When he walked into the building, Tom put up his hands and said, "This place is really affluent and prosperous."

This is a technology that all of us can use: you can read with your hands and with other parts of your anatomy, and you can use the amplified mind.

"How can you know that?" someone asked him.

"I can feel it," said Tom. "Everything has a vibratory correlate. Everything has energy. I can pick it up through the pores of my skin."

It's true for you too. You can walk into an environment and tell whether the vibes are good or bad. Is there anyone who hasn't felt vibes in that way?

At one point Tom met the great golfer Arnold Palmer. He shook his hand and said, "Arnie, I've always wanted to meet you. I'm a great fan of yours. I love watching you golf. Beyond that, I want to golf with you."

Arnie said, "I've never golfed with anyone blind. I'd be delighted to golf with you."

"But Arnie," said Tom, "I've got to tell you something. I'm a gambler. I want to bet you $1,000 a hole that I can whip you."

"Tom," said Arnie, "I've been golfing a long time. I have to tell you I'm really good. I do this vocationally and avocationally. I feel bad about taking your money."

"I insist: $1,000 a hole," said Tom. "Let's shake on it."

"Great. Anytime, anywhere."

"Tonight at midnight."

Your Name Has Value

Arnold Palmer did extremely well. His agent Mark McCormack parlayed his name into a fortune. Arnie netted $100 million for putting his name on golf balls, sports equipment, clothes at Sears, and Rolex watches. Rolex was paying him $3 million for a commercial that was going to take less than three hours. The Rolex chairman said, "$3 million for three hours. Don't you think he could give us a little more than that?"

"He doesn't need to," said McCormack. "He's built his name, and we're going to bring Rolex's name up with Arnold Palmer's name. It's not the other way around. If you want me to tear up the check and not have him do it, that's OK." In sales, that is called a takeaway close!

Right now, say, *My name has value.*

When you decide to fine-tune yourself, you're born rich. Your eighty-six billion brain cells come to work. The more you visualize, the easier it is, the faster and the more clearly and cleanly it unfolds, and the more energy that comes to you to facilitates all the dreams you've been dreaming. That's why the rich get richer.

Gerald Jampolsky is a physician who's written a book called *Love Is Letting Go of Fear.* That's really what it's about. If you have enough love, it conquers everything. Gerald has an institute in Tiburon, California, called the Center for Attitudinal Healing, and he works with terminally ill kids. He does it all out of the tenderness of his heart, because he understands that if you just be good and do good, and good comes back to you karmically. Jerry was a drug user and an alcoholic and reformed himself by changing the pictures in his mind. Visualizing is realizing. You can go from where you are to anywhere if you're ready.

Right now, say, *I'm ready.*

Also say, *I'm giving myself new levels of permission, and I like and accept myself the way I am now.*

God Will Provide

I believe that Mother Teresa, as suggested above, was one of the most cosmically conscious people on the planet. During a visit to the United States, she went to San Quentin State Prison in California. She took a giant white chart, drew one black dot on it, and said, "Gentlemen, the little dot is this besmirchment from what you've done against society. The white is all the infinite potential that is left on a canvas called your life."

Someone who's changed the pictures in his mind is my friend Dr. Louis Tartaglia. He and I are mastermind partners. He generates future visions that manifest at such quick rates that I can't fathom it.

Louis wanted to go to India, but he had no visible source of supply. Although he does well as a psychiatrist, he does lots of philanthropy and doesn't have any excess funds. Then I introduced him to Del Smith of Evergreen Airlines, who said, "We own Air India and a few other things. We'll just fly you from New York to India."

We helped Louis meet all the right people. One person he very much wanted to meet was Mother Teresa. He had it in his mind that he was going to meet her no matter what, even though he'd written letters to her and never gotten a reply.

Louis gets to Mother Teresa's headquarters in Calcutta. The first thing the head sister tells him is, "I'm sorry. Mother Teresa has been sick for the last week, and unfortunately nobody is able to meet with her now. We sent you a letter saying that there was no chance you could get on her schedule, although it seems you didn't get it."

As Louis is talking to the sister, all of a sudden he hears a gentle, almost fragile voice from a lady coming down the hall. Everyone's attention is galvanized, because it's Mother Teresa. She's come to tell the head sister that one of the brothers needs to have somebody that can speak Italian and do some work with the Twelve-Step program.

Mother Teresa kept saying, "Don't worry, God will provide."

Louis Tartaglia finished his medical doctorate and did postgraduate work in Italy. He's just standing there, basking in her presence, and he's joy-filled. "Mother Teresa," he says, "you haven't met me; I'm Dr. Louis Tartaglia. I'm the psychiatrist who wrote you a letter, and I understand that you couldn't meet with me. I happen to speak eloquent Italian. I'd love to help you with the Twelve-Step program."

"I told you God will provide," she says.

Getting your visualization working is only half of it. I want you to be crystal clear that that's not the whole show. The other half is that the universe is outpicturing some programs of its own. The goal is to be in the flow—tuned in, turned on, and proceeding in the direction of your desires so that you are unstoppable. When you're in the flow, your good will show up.

Good in Pictures of Bad

Sometimes your good comes in a picture of bad. You say, "Wait a second. This isn't what I outpictured, and this isn't what I want." If you start claiming it as bad, it will stay bad, even though it was going to develop into good. If I'd said, "Poor me. I'm bankrupt, and I'm never going to make it," I would have stayed locked in that, but if you look up, you go up.

That's why it says without vision, we perish. With vision, you flourish.

Back in 1927, Bucky Fuller's daughter died of spinal meningitis. He's at the end of the pier and Lake Michigan, ready to jump into the blue and end it all.

He knows that his wife can go back to her family. Her father is wealthy; Hewlett, Long Island, is named after him. He wouldn't give this Yankee tinkerer any money, because he knew Bucky would waste it. He was just a tinkerer, and his mind was on stupid ideas. He was wasting the family's money, so the old man cut him off.

Bucky thought, "If I kill myself, at least Anne and our second daughter, Allegra, will be taken care of."

He was ready to jump off, and suddenly two questions filtered into his mind. Number one, is there a God? The answer was spontaneous: "There is an a priori intelligence in the universe." Second question, "Do I have a reason to be alive?" The spontaneous response was, "I'm here for humanity's comprehensive welfare on Spaceship Earth."

"I could have come up with a magic flying slipper," he said, "but it didn't seem right, seeing that the more I went into history, the more I could go into the future."

As I told my brother once when we were talking about our childhood, you can't go forward until you know what's been behind you in this time frame.

We need to be looking forward in order to go forward, but in order to look forward, we've got to understand where we've been. I'm going to show you how to do that.

The point of the whole trip is to make it fun all the time. You're going to have situations that don't look right, but as the Bible says, "Judge not by the appearance" (John 7:24).

That includes facts. You may say, "But the fact is I don't have any money." Dr. Tartaglia didn't have any way to see Mother Teresa. It doesn't matter what the fact is; your mind creates all.

There is a pattern going in universe that you may not have created, but you can get synchro-meshed with it and manifest the good that you desire—if you're ready.

Right now say, *I'm ready.*

You can do it in an incredibly short time, because you can say:

My life is clicking.

My wealth is clicking.

My health is clicking.

My joy is clicking.

My happiness is clicking.

My peacefulness is clicking.

My good is unlimited.

It doesn't really matter how you arrive at something; it matters that you put your thought out. In his book *The Magic of Believing*, Claude Bristol calls it a thought projection: you send out your thought projection out with linearity.

Little kids are so smart, because they know the biblical law, "Ask and you shall receive," but they don't believe in deferred gratification. What do they do? Ask, ask, ask.

Once when my daughter was little, we were walking hand in hand over to her best friend's house. She looked up at me and says, "Daddy, if you're really, really nice, and say please, I'll let you carry me."

My daughter is smart in two languages, because our housekeeper when she was growing up spoke great Spanish, as does my wife. She grew up thinking that it's normal and natural to speak more than one language. I believe that every kid should grow up bilingual, but it ought to be part of an organic whole, because before age twelve, language is easy. After the age of twelve, we've all been lied to and told it is hard, so it becomes hard. We wait until a guy or girl goes to college and say, "Now it's time to learn a language so you can get a bachelor of arts degree and you can graduate in liberal arts and sciences."

We're spending the money at the wrong time. We spend tens of thousands of dollars on each college education. It would be much better to spend that money at an earlier age. According to Dr. Benjamin Bloom's research at University of Chicago, your IQ is 70 to 80 percent set by the time you're seven or eight years old. That being true, what you want to do is max out kids' experiences. The pioneering educator Maria Montessori started the concept of experiential learning: basically, if you learn it by experience, you know it.

I failed geometry in high school. Now I've got a master's degree in comprehensive anticipatory design science, meaning I know the geometry of the universe, called *synergetics*. Bucky wrote a bestselling book with this title and taught to the subject to us. It's easy. Bucky said, "I won't teach you anything that a nine-year-old can't experience and put together, red to red, blue to blue, based on triangulation, which is the center and start of all of the universe."

Bucky saw these principles in his mind because he was nearsighted and nearly blind from birth. When he was born in 1895, ophthalmology was in its infancy. He had gigantic binoculars for glasses. He said, "I could never see, so when I had clay, I made models, and the models that would stay together were based on triangles. I thought that must have something to do with the universe. I penetrated the metaphysical mustiness, and I came out with the mathematics called synergetics—the behavior of whole systems, which is unpredictable by its parts or subassemblies." Bucky coined the word *synergy* in 1943.

I used to drive Bucky home at 2:30 in the morning. It used to enervate me, because he'd say, "Pick me at up at 4:30." I'd think, "I'm one-third of this guy's age, and I can't believe he said that." Bucky only slept two hours per night, because he felt he wanted to serve humanity. He had cut his sleep cycles by a minute a night until he got to the bottom of two hours, which is all he needed to be fully and completely functioning.

This goes to the next principle: never say you're tired until right before you're ready to go to sleep. Most people say, "Oh, my God. I'm not going to get enough sleep tonight. I'm going to feel miserable." That's bad affirming, because affirmations are things that you say to yourself or that others say to you that you think about, act upon, and let act upon you. People badmouth themselves, and when the bad result shows up, they're amazed. Wrong affirmation, wrong result.

Bucky would say, "I'm going to go instantly into deep sleep, and when I wake up, I'm waking up refreshed." Why would you ever give yourself anything else?

When I joined the speaking business, my motivational mentor, Cavett Robert, said, "You're going to miss a lot of meals." It doesn't matter if my body misses a few, because I believe in the see-food diet: if I see it, I eat it. He also said, "You're going to miss some serious amounts of sleep, because sometimes you've got no choice: you take the red-eye and or you drive all night." Both of which were true.

Once I was driving Bucky and I said to him, "Do you meditate?" He said, "Don't you understand? I live in meditation. Mark, the universe isn't here to serve you. You're here to serve the universe."

Today the prevailing attitude is that life owes me a living. But there's only one person that's supposed to take care of you. Who is that?

You.

You may say, "Wait a second. I'm supposed to take care of my spouse." If you can do that, then God bless. Let's have an umbrella; let's do the best we can, but when you shut your eyes, you're in there alone. Let's do a better job.

Five

Relaxed Awakeness

Now what are the rules? What are the programs for creative visualization?

The first step is *relaxed awakeness*. This is where you do your deep breathing, your closed-eye processing. You close your eyes. You go into your inner eye, into the theater of your mind. You see things the way you want to see them rather than the way they are.

One of the great writers in this field is Neville Goddard, who usually just went by "Neville." I highly recommend Neville's *Resurrection*, which is about visualization; I've read it over a hundred times. He touches my heart in a marvelous way. There's not a page in my copy that's not heavily highlighted with yellow colored marks, because he's taught me so much. I've got his autographed picture behind my desk; I paid a fortune for it because I said, "This guy just knew and was blissfully wise." He turned me on to this line in Isaiah, which I'd never understood before: "And it shall come to pass, that before they call, I will answer; and while they are yet speaking, I will hear" (Isaiah 65:24).

That's God talking—"I will answer"—but God's only in one place, and that's in you. You're on the mountaintop of your own experience. You say, "I want it"; God says, "You want it, you shall have it."

How do you get to that state? What did Christ say? "When thou pray, enter into thy secret closet, and when thou hast shut thy door, pray to your Father" (Matthew 6:6). What are you shutting the door on? You're shutting the door on lack. You're shutting the door on doubt. You're shutting the door on fear. You're shutting the door on low-mindedness. You're shutting the door on what you *can't* be, do, or have. You're shutting the door on yesterday, and you're thinking in the now, because the only time your subconscious works is in the eternal now.

You go inside this wondrous state of relaxed awakeness. If you were in India, they would show you how to do the lotus position and raise your hands up to the sun. But posture is not that important. If you're going to learn how to do what I'm about to teach you, you might want to think about being in a recliner or being reclined right before you go to sleep. The principle here is that you need a state of controlled reverie, controlled imagination.

Disengage yourself from all external stimuli, meaning that I hope the phone doesn't ring while you're doing this; I hope the kids don't cry and your significant other has had their needs satiated beforehand.

You want to have a smile on your face. That's very important. That's why it says in the Bible, "Let not the sun go down upon your wrath" (Ephesians 4:26). If you go to bed in a grumpy, angry, hostile mood, when you wake up, you're going to feel the same way or worse. Why? Because the subconscious never sleeps. Someone over in China who's also thinking awful thoughts adds to yours, and you feel more awful, because there's only one mind. It's as if there's one main computer, of which you and I are little branches. We're minis coming off the maxi.

In any case, always go into meditation with a smile. If you really want to get high, tilt your closed eyes up at a forty-five-degree angle. When Bucky Fuller spoke at class graduations, he'd talk for three or four hours. People would be telling the president of the school, "Get him out of here. These people have to graduate." Bucky would be talking profoundly about the universe. When he closed his eyes, tilted them up, and had his hands in an Indian namaste "Bless the spirit within you" gesture, he would talk extemporaneously and unceasingly. The only reason he'd get off was to go to the bathroom.

Biofeedback technology shows that when you tilt your inner eyes up, you go into an instant alpha state, which is the most creative of the four vibratory countenances of consciousness.

Which is where you want to stay.

You may say, "It hurts me to tilt my eyes up." Yeah, anything new is uncomfortable. If you go for a long trip on a bicycle on your first day, your calves are going to ache when you get back, but you get used to it. I'm so used to it, I've got nineteen-inch calves.

Living on a Bike
When I was nine, my parents took my brothers and me on a trip to Europe. While we were there, we got to see bicycle races. I had never seen such a thing because at that time we didn't have them in this country.

Over there they had racing bicycles with low curved handlebars. Today everyone's got them, but back in 1957, nobody in America had them yet. I wanted one of these with all my head and heart. When we were going through England, I cut the picture of the bike I want out of a magazine: "Ride a Wheel on Sheffield Steel." It cost $175.

When I got home, I put this picture on the wall next to my bed. I said, "That's my bicycle." I kept hitting on my father to buy it for me. He said, "Great, boy. You can have it when you're twenty-one and can make your own decisions."

"You don't understand," I said. "I want it now." Little kids know no better than to keep asking. I got him down to sixteen, but that was as low as I could get him to go chronologically.

I wanted that bike fiercely. Every night I would go to bed and look at that picture. I was reading *Cycling* magazine. I'd close my eyes, and I could see myself being one of the Windy City Wheelmen in Chicago, who would bicycle four hundred miles a day. I said, "Not only am I going to have this bicycle, but I'm going to have one of those DayGlo jerseys. I'm going to win, and it's going to be just magnificent."

I knew that I was supposed to be a bicyclist and a racer. I didn't know why; I just knew that I was. I kept asking my Dad. Finally, I said, "Dad, can I have it if I earn it myself?"

If you have a nine-year-old son, do you believe he could earn $1,614 (in today's dollars) by himself in six months? My dad was convinced I couldn't earn that amount back then.

I read in *Boy Scout Life* magazine that you could sell Christmas cards on consignment. So I got some Christmas cards. I was in Waukegan, Illinois, where the snow is deep in November and early December. I had a blue parka, a cold, red face, and big, furry mittens, and I would come up and ring people's doorbells.

The woman who answered would look at me and say, "Young man, come in here. I've got to blow your nose." Now in sales, when the attention goes, the energy flows; whatever you recognize, you energize. So I'm home free. When we're done playing "Let's blow the little kid's nose," I say, "I'm earning my own bicycle. Would you like to invest in one box of Christmas cards or two?"

In sales, after you make a closing statement, you shut up. I sold 376 boxes of Christmas cards in one month. Did I want to sell that many Christmas cards? Did I want to be the number one greeting card salesman in the nine-year-old division of North America?

No; I wanted a bicycle. Where was it created? The cause was in my mind; the result was the bike. It all started because I was living on that bike. I felt like a bicyclist. I was coming out of mastery, being a Windy City Wheelman, with the appropriate attire, and doing it all before it happened.

Changing Our Eyescape

My optometrist, Donald Harris, of Newport Beach, California, used exactly the same principle. He said, "There's got to be a way to get people out of wearing glasses, whether they're nearsighted, farsighted, or astigmatic."

That was important to me, because by the time I was four years old, I was so nearsighted I was crashing into things. My parents very lovingly took me to an optometrist in Waukegan. He gave me bottle-thick glasses, the kind that made your eyes look bigger than the glasses. At sixteen, I got my first set of contact lenses, and I was thankful.

For years, Donald Harris kept saying, "There's got to be a way to get people out of glasses without invasive surgery." With a couple of his partners, he came up with the process that they patented called orthokeratology, Ortho-K. It's a contact lens that works on your cornea the way braces work on teeth: they reshape the cornea.

Is that important to you and me? Yeah, because the prevailing belief is—and beliefs always crystallize our reality—that after age forty, your eyes get worse. That's not true. It's just a belief system; you inpicture it so you outpicture it. You've got to be careful, because many of the things that have dominion over you are simply belief systems.

The good thing is you own your own capacity to create your belief system. The creator is always greater than the creation. Just because it's been that way doesn't mean it's got to be that way. By reshaping corneas, Donald Harris is changing our eye scape.

We're going to have breakthroughs at absolutely every level of the human body, so we can get rid of all the things that we currently call problems. Dr. Jonas Salk got rid of polio, just as we got rid of smallpox.

Every one of those diseases will be cured by somebody who goes into their imaginal realm to create a new cure and solve the problem for a profit. As I've said, IQ is irrelevant. It measures where we've been, not where we can go. Because what is inside each one of us is pure potential.

Right now, say, *My potential is infinite and I am on-purpose to use it to fulfill my destiny.*

How to Cut It in the Big World

You may know this guy's story, but I think it may demonstrate these point better than any others. He was born in New York's Hell's Kitchen. His father was into child abuse. He could have said, "Oh, poor me. Everybody's always beating up on me," but he didn't. He was kicked out of eleven high schools as incorrigible. They tested him at Drexel University, discovered he had the awesome IQ of under ninety, and wrote a letter that said, "You will be lucky to become an elevator operator," which he has framed and hung in his home today.

He goes in school to Switzerland, comes back as a character actor, and fails night after night after night in New York. One night, he is watching Muhammad Ali on TV, and it hits his hot button. He said, "That's it. I could write a screenplay that shows American honor, dignity, courage, valor, and higher principles." He said, "I can do it, and because I can, I will do it."

He locked himself in his room for three days, put black paper on the windows, and practiced what we call *channeling*. He wrote the script as directed, and it came out letter-perfect. He went to Hollywood to sell it. The first guy who read it said, "Yeah, this is great. Here's a check for 300 grand. Now buzz off."

"Whoa," said this guy. "You don't understand the program. If I'm not the lead player in the script, you don't get my script. Here's your check back."

He found a little investment group, got $1 million together, and made the movie. They made $100 million on it. The film was *Rocky*. The guy's name is Sylvester Stallone. He owned 20 percent of it for authorship and acting in it and became phenomenally successful with sequels and prequels.

Another movie, *Amadeus*, is about Wolfgang Amadeus Mozart. His father always said, "You are a musical genius," so he became a musical genius. If you're going to affirm your kids, affirm them positively. Brag them up, don't drag them down verbally, emotionally or intellectually. See more in them than they see in themselves. "Everyone is born a genius," according to Bucky Fuller. Please don't call them idiots or stupid or clumsy or klutzy.

Stallone changed his affirmation. He said, "I could write this script." Newscaster Barbara Walters interviewed Sylvester Stallone multiple times. She said, "Most people think he is dumb. Not only is he not dumb, but he is the smartest mind I've ever met." The guy's colossally good because he keeps telling himself, "I'm good."

There's no payoff in bad-mouthing yourself or letting somebody else bad-mouth you and buying into it. Look at one of the lines Stallone wrote in *Rocky 1*. He asks the coach, "How do I cut it in the big world?"

The coach said, "You've got to eat lightning and crap thunder." There's no way to miss the intent of that line.

Controlled Reverie

Begin by going into relaxed awakeness; then use controlled reverie. You close your outer eyes and go inside the theater of your mind. Whom do you see in there? You.

You can prelive your agenda. You see it as reality with finesse and panache before it comes to pass. Say, "I call those things that are not seen as though they were seen, and the things that were not seen became seen." Isn't that what Christ said? Use your inner eye. He said, "Many have eyes but cannot see."

That sounds like gobbledygook. How could someone have eyes and not see? Because they're looking at external reality. I'm going to show you how to penetrate that and get inside. You'll get the real insight so you can be out of sight.

At our best, we are superb, excellent, extraordinary. Most of us have far poorer models for ourselves. If you watch the news media every night, most of it's bad. If you read the newspaper, take a red pen and check off the negative stories versus the positive ones; you'll see that they're 90 percent negative. Therefore limit negative news inputs to fifteen minutes or less a day, or you'll inadvertently pollute your spirit, mind, and body.

All of us know how to visualize, whether we know it or not, but most of us are masters at negative visualization: we're full of worry. Worry is thinking in our mind's eye what's not working, without doing anything but worrying. It's a one-way elevator going down. If somebody say something's going wrong, most of us zoom and lock right in on it. If somebody tells you something's going to be colossally good, what do we say? "That's too good to be true." It's only too good to be true because you haven't patterned your mind to assume that the best is going to happen to you all the time.

Right now, say, *The best is going to happen to me all the time.*

Some might say that's Pollyannaish. Businessman and author W. Clement Stone was predeceased by his wife and both his kids. His son had been running his corporation, which was called Combined Insurance. Someone said to him, "How can everything that happens to you be positive? Your son just got kissed out of life at age fifty-six."

Stone said, "I'm happy for my son. He led a full, rich, majestic life. I think he smelled the roses. I think he created a great family. I think he was a great man and did a good job, but his heart just wasn't as strong as his mind muscle, and he's gone."

"Do you want to tell me what's good about that?"

"I'm sad that I lost my son. I'm happy that it forced me to come out of retirement; now, at eighty-four, I've recreated the corporation into Aon Corporation. We do $5.4 billion worth of business a year. I'm here to make the world better for this and all future generations. If my son had not died, I wouldn't have come back to work."

Once I told this story at a seminar. Afterward a mother came up to me and said, "My son just ripped me off and left, and now I've got to run the corporation again. Until you told that story about Stone, I didn't think I had the power to go out and do it all over again, but if he can do it at his age, then I can certainly do it at my age."

Visualize Backwards

One of my heroes, Neville, said, "If you really want to learn visualization, learn it backwards. When you go to sleep, visualize every second, every nanosecond, going backwards, that is, visualize backwards. From the time you're going to bed, visualize kissing the kids if you've got some, or whomever you're kissing goodnight, going back in through the kitchen, to eating the meal, through your day at work if that's where you work, through going to work all the way to sunsight." (Bucky said, "The sun doesn't rise: you have a sunsight.") Clean up the day so that when you start the next day, you start fresh and clean.

Visualizing backwards facilitates your going forward. It's the same thing I said about Bucky: to be a prober, to visualize fifty years in advance, you've got to know history comprehensively.

How to Correct Your Day

You can also visualize the day, not as it was, but as corrected. That's why it's never too late to have a happy childhood. All you've got now is the idea of what you experienced. You can go back and mentally eradicate, say, a conflict between you and your mom. Whatever that conflict was, go back one mini-episode at a time and re-edit it, re-direct it, re-script it. You've got all the power in your mind to have your mom say anything you want: "Oh, I love you, darling. You're the most wonderful thing," instead of "You SOB, I hate you. You're no good."

Just change it to "You're lovable, effervescent, joyous. You are the joy of my heart. You just warm the cockles of my heart. You're the sweetest daughter anybody could ever have." Mom doesn't have any control over this, does she?

Until you correct it, you have to keep re-living it. Every one of your thoughts is a videotape, and it's on constant re-run; it's on continuous loop. That's why it's never stopped. It just keeps going and going. The thought keeps going in your head until you change it.

Once in a while, you have anger about something. I was talking to somebody, and all of a sudden I found out I was really hostile toward the person we were talking about; I didn't know I had that much anger. I said, "Right now, I'm going to release it." Because the only time you can forgive anyone is right now. The only time you can forgive yourself is right now.

Choose to practice radical forgiveness, and watch your life transform brilliantly and almost instantly before your eyes. Forgiveness works, because love only has two aspects: givingness and forgivingness.

You can do this visualizing backwards anytime, but it's best to do it right before you go to sleep at night, simply because you've got to shut down your external senses then. You've got to unplug. It is best to be undisturbed and in "the secret place of the Most High" (Psalm 91:1).

Right now, use your hands as if they're plugged into an electric socket. Then unplug them and say, *I'm unplugging.*

You've got to unplug your physical sensations so you can go into your deeper sensation, the creative tissue fabric of experience because everything is out-pictured by the mind. If you're reading this idea for the first time, it can be hard to buy into, but the more you look into this process, the faster the mind creates.

Six

Come from the End Result

Once I took my car in to get a $30 oil change. The mechanic checked it out and said, "This is going to cost you almost $800 before you leave here."

"I thought I was just getting the oil changed," I said.

"Yeah, but you've got an oil leak. You've go this; you've got that. You need new this and that."

It was a relatively new car, and I thought, "I need all that? I just wanted to pay $30 for the oil change."

I could have let that ruin my whole day. The point is that you're going to get sidetracked through life. Whatever happens, claim, "That's good."

This is tough stuff, because $800 is real money. But I still get to create my reality. I said, "OK. That's fine."

The next day, I went to pick up the car, and somehow the door is broken. Now I needed a new door handle. The mechanic said, "It'll take another day."

"You didn't tell me it was going to take another day," I said. "I haven't got another day. I keep things in my car. I have the best roving tape library around. This is my classroom on wheels. I've got to have it locked, and I don't want anything stolen out of it. I know how to put white light around it, but I don't want anything stolen."

"It'll still take you a day."

"That's good, that's good. I'm thankful. That's good."

When he had it fixed it up, I had to drive up to LA that afternoon. The car would not go past sixty miles an hour, no matter what I did. I called up the mechanic.

Incidentally, here are the people whose cell phone numbers you've got to get. You've got to have the numbers of your medical doctor, your chiropractor, your attorney, your accountant, and your mechanic. You may think they won't give them to you, but they will, because you don't deal in life

normally anymore. You're going to have above average relations. Average relations are below average.
That means you're going to befriend them. You're
going to talk to them eyeball-to-eyeball. You're going
to shake them. You're going to congratulate them.
When they do something right for you, give them
a dozen long-stemmed chocolate chip cookies. Do
something novel. If you want to get rich, come up
with a novel thing to give people.

In any case, I called the mechanic. He said,
"Bring it in tomorrow." I said, "I've got to be down
in San Diego for a 10:00 talk, and I've got to leave
early."

"I'll meet you at 7:30," he said.

When I brought the car in, the mechanic said,
"When we steam-cleaned your engine, water obvi-
ously got on the turbocharger, and that's the problem."

He fixed it. Now I'm in the car going down the
405 to San Diego, and I've got a bunch of people
waiting for me. Now my car's only going forty miles
an hour and I think, "Oh, my God. What am I going
to do? It got worse; it didn't get better."

Jack Boland, author of *The Master Mind Principle*, says you have to marvel at the marveling.
Decide that everything is marvelous. This seems
cuckoo, right?

I've got all these people waiting, and I'm not going to make it. I've done what I was supposed to do. I want to bad-mouth the mechanic, but I say, "This is marvelous. There's a great benefit hidden in here, if I only look and stay awake."

In Mission Viejo, I see a Mercedes dealership, and I wheel my car in. There's nobody in there but me. A guy bounces out like a jackrabbit, opens my door, and says, "How can I be of service to you?" This guy has his hand in mine—my seatbelt isn't unbuckled yet—and he's pulling me up. He's elevating me with a great smile.

I say, "I don't know who's trained you, but you are trained way better than average. This should be your place."

"It will be soon," he says.

"Look," I say, "I've got one of the best servicemen in the world. Chris does a great job. I just spent almost $800 fixing this little deal, and yesterday it wouldn't go past sixty; now it won't go past forty. I've got an important meeting down in San Diego, and it would mean a lot to me and to hundreds of folks if I could get there. Could you see your way clear to make this thing work?"

"Chris is your guy?" he says.

"Chris is my guy."

"Chris is my best friend." Marvel at the marveling; don't worry; be happy. "We'll just call and see what he did and didn't do. It must be something simple."

"Thank you, Father," I say.

This mechanic calls up Chris, who says, "Look, we think we did everything."

Now the service manager is there. I'm bouncing up and down, giving him a book and making him my friend as fast as I possibly can. You've got to give before you can receive. You've got to be prayed up in the universe, and I think I'm pretty well prayed up. You've got to cover every base, because you want to keep marveling at the marveling.

The mechanic says, "I think it's just the air filters. They should get changed every fifteen thousand miles, but we've got a lot of polluted air on the highways, where you're sitting in traffic jams."

"That's true."

"We've got a lot of cars before you."

"That's true," I say. "I wouldn't normally ask to go to the head of the line, but I'll bet you, being the head of this great operation, could do that, couldn't you?"

"Normally we'd want your car for hours."

"I haven't got hours. Here's my problem. I bet you could solve it, couldn't you?"

"I could, in fifteen minutes." It took him sixty minutes exactly, and he said, "It'd probably be $75, but for you, $30." Marvel at the marveling.

As I've said, when visualizing, start by going into relaxed awakeness. Then go inside the theater of your mind. Finally, come from the end result.

From is the critical word here. Don't think about it, wish about it, hope about it. Remember, practice doesn't make perfect. Perfect practice makes perfect. Olympic gold medalist Mary Lou Retton went over her gymnastics routine over and over. "I see myself going through every motion letter-perfect," she said. "I see myself coming off the high bars victoriously and valiantly. I see Mama coming unglued out of her chair, tears streaming through her mascara. I see the digital clock read out a perfect ten. I see the audience giving me a tumultuous standing ovation. I see a contract from Wheaties for $3 million." She succeeded with elegance and precision. Function from the end result.

Had she won before she got there? Yes.

Today, with the advent of inexpensive video equipment, we can all record ourselves doing what we want to do and watch the video only when it's perfect.

As one swimming coach said, "We're in the time of high tech, but we've got to have commensurate high touch." He has his divers watching their own perfect dives for two hours every morning. He never shows them what they did wrong. Why? Drill, practice, and rehearse. Go over it and over it and over it. When we're teaching little kids, what do we do? We do it again and again and again. Then as adults, we say, "I'll lock in the first time and have it forever." It doesn't work that way.

You may ask, "Does this only operate in sports?" No, it operates everywhere. It operates because your mind is a video recorder. Every one of your brain cells is a video replete with emotion and information, just like holographic images.

Ways to Part Reality

The first time I got to deal with special-ed kids, I was invited to come to a place in the middle of Wisconsin. I had to fly to Milwaukee and drive forever to get to this little ranch.

When I arrived, one of the special-ed kids sauntered in an awkward body up to the car. He opened the door. He was slobbering all over himself and then he decided to hug me.

(At that time, I wasn't into teaching hugging, and I didn't understand that everyone has a tactile need.)

I got to meet all of the kids and talk to them. I was impressed by Victor, the man who started this place. He had a kid with Down syndrome, but he said, "Look. I'm not going to buy into the kid having Down syndrome. There's got to be a way to break through." All of a sudden, he found out that his kid dealt with animals at a vibratory level that no normal human being could. The worst dog in the neighborhood would come up and this kid could pet him and hug him, because the dog perceived no threat, no vibratory resistance.

Victor started bringing in ferocious felines. Then, all of a sudden, the word went out that he was taking care of these animals, and it got out to other parents of Down syndrome children—because there's only one mind.

The word should go through you rather than returning to the void. You go out and accomplish the mission and prosper positively or negatively instead of doing. Word goes out. All the other parents bring their kids with Down syndrome to Victor, saying, "Will you take my kid?" All of a sudden he ends up with a gigantic ranch. Now they're feeding and breeding ferocious animals that could never have been bred in captivity before.

These kids walk up to black panthers, cougars, and other ferocious animals and pet and cuddle and kiss and roll around with them. The kids are hand-feeding these animals.

The janitor who was monitoring all this assumed that all these animals must be docile and tame. When I met him, he had no right arm, because they had decided that his vibratory rate was certainly not that of a kid with Down syndrome.

What am I saying? There are ways to part reality, and the way to do it starts with the imagination. We've got problems, but as I learned from W. Clement Stone and Norman Vincent Peale, the problems have got to be seen as good.

As long as you pronounce them as bad, they become bad. If you pronounce them as good, at least you're awake to the new possibilities. One of my favorite poets, Retsama, talks about self-mastery:

> I, at last, have reached the goal and solved the mystery of my soul. I am that to which I pray, that to which I look for aid. I am that which I did seek, I am my own mountain peak. I, upon creation, look as if a leaf in my own book. For I, the one, the many make of substance which from me I take. For all is me, there are no two. Creation is myself all through.

The Five Inner Senses

If you're the one creating your experience of whom you bring into your experience and whom you send out of your experience, why not do more mind work? That's where it all starts—in your mind— and it starts with our five senses.

We've got five interior senses to go with our five exterior senses. The first one is your inner eye. See yourself as you want to be. If you've got to go to a bank, see yourself getting a loan. If you go to the doctor, hear your doctor with your inner ear pronouncing you as healthy. Get into the inner feeling. If you're going to have a feeling, have a good feeling. I recommend that on the way home from work, you listen to romantic music like that of Lionel Richie or Neil Diamond, but on the way to work, listen to my audio recordings or something else that winds your clock.

You may have clear hearing: clairaudience. You can be on the phone and know after three or four words who's at the other end of the phone.

You may want to hear something said to you like, "Congratulations, you're a millionaire." Who is it that would tell you that? Your spouse, your banker, your broker, your realtor? Somebody's going to tell you that. Imagine that voice and keep running that scenario in your mind until it's got some reality to it.

Your inner sense of smell—do I smell my home environment before I get there? You bet. I want everything around me smelling good. We can make a fundamental difference and change the whole ecology. I really believe that every one of us ought to plant one tree a year for the rest of our lives. I do more than my share, but I'd like the rest of the world to understand that that is just good ecology.

Yes, somebody else is going to sit under the shade of the tree you planted. You and I are sitting in front of the shade of other people's trees, so why shouldn't we make the same thing possible for others? Others have paved the roads you and I are traveling and dug the wells we're drinking at. We've got to do it for those who will come after us, just as those who came before did it for us. Why not see how good we can make the whole opportunity?

You may say, "I don't have any inner sense of taste." But have you have ever been to a restaurant where you haven't smelled or tasted the food, but your whole mouth is already wet with anticipation. What a sensual experience!

Once I was taken to a first-rate restaurant. We went in, and the maître d' was everything you'd want of a polished European. He loved to serve. He didn't say thank-you; he said, "It's my pleasure to serve you," and he bowed with great dignity and class; you knew that he meant it, because this was the right vocation for him. As he talked about the food and put romance into it, we couldn't smell anything yet, but our salivary glands were already at work. That's what inner taste is. Why not convert some of it into the best tastes that exist at all levels?

Lessons from Della Reese

I want to tell two stories that summarize these principles. They're about the late singer Della Reese, whom I loved a great deal.

Years ago, Della gets a call from her agency to fill in for another celebrity; I think it's in Acapulco. She's all packed and ready to go, and she's waiting for the phone call to find out who's picking her up. She's sitting out in the sun at her swimming pool with her eight-year-old daughter, Della Reese Jr., who nicknamed herself Dumsy.

Dumsy had not told Della that she'd shut the sliding glass door on the way out of the house. Now Della is a woman of great physical substance. She hears the phone ring, and she starts moving like a locomotive, not seeing that the glass door is shut, and crashes headfirst through the glass door, falling over the glass, and essentially carving herself in half. She later said, "Out of nowhere, God's hand came, picked up my head, and when it did, all the glass came careening down from on high." Otherwise the falling glass would have effectively served as a guillotine.

Now she's bleeding to death. She sees a towel, and she immediately puts a tourniquet on herself. (This was right before 911 came into existence.) Dumsy has nowhere to call, so she runs a mile and a half to the doctor's house. It's Sunday afternoon, and he's watching football. She walks in unannounced. Talk about perfect one-minute management and one-minute goal-setting and one-minute demand—this guy's sitting in his BVDs, drinking beer, watching football. She grabs him by the britches and says, "We're moving out, and I mean right now. Mama's bleeding to death. Grab your black bag en route."

The doctor goes back with Dumsy, and sees Della has lost eight of nine operating pints of blood—she's technically dead. The first thing he does is regurgitate, then he recovers his senses and calls an ambulance. The ambulance comes and takes her to the hospital.

Now you never die without your own permission, as my late client and friend Dr. Elisabeth Kübler-Ross used to teach.

Della Reese arrives at the hospital. She is technically dead. She is on a gurney, and they're arguing about who's going to sign her in, because they say an eight-year-old can't do that.

Now Della is outside the body, looking down on the inanity of our hospital system, which is worried about who's going to take care of fiduciary responsibility. She sits up, scaring the bejesus out of the nurse, grabs the charts, and says, "Look. I'm over twenty-one. I'll sign me in now. Let's go operate and quit goofing around."

She is being anesthetized to be operated on. The doctors are saying, "We're going to have to lop off her leg. We didn't have anybody sign permission for that."

If you talk to any anesthetist, they'll say this is technically not possible, but Della takes off the anesthetic mask. She sits up—perfect one-minute management. She looks around at all the doctors one at a time, says, "You guys are better than you think you are. Now the big guy and I have been talking. That leg stays, and you put it back on. That leg look good, don't it?" Her grammar may have been inaccurate, but she got to keep her leg.

Let me do a quick aside here. Do not let yourself go under the scalpel of a doctor who may bad-mouth you when you are anesthetized. Your subconscious never sleeps. It's always awake; it's always listening.

Recent research out of Sweden says if the doctors bad-mouth you while you're under anesthetic, you're less likely to heal and may even die. If they're neutral and talk about golfing or something else while you're under, you heal normally. If they say, "This is going to be an easy operation, a piece of cake," you will have a fast and exquisitely good healing, because you were under somebody else's authority and tutelage, and you believed their suggestion.

Make sure you have positive doctors, because a lot of them have been drinking their own bath-water. They go straight into medical school and start buying into the idea that they are closer to God than anyone else and have knowledge that nobody else has.

Another time, Della is on Johnny Carson's *Tonight Show*, and she has an aneurysm, a blood clot on the brain. Twenty-eight neurosurgeons at the Beverly Hills hospital come in to see her. All of them want to have her sign a document saying, "Your estate will not sue me, or my estate, because there's a 98 percent chance you're not going to get up off the operating table."

Would you want to be operated on by a physician like that? No way. Neither did she. She fired every one of them. Her husband Franklin says, "Della, you just fired the last guy available in Southern California."

"Well, then bring that boy back here."

The doctor comes in and says, "Yes, Miss Reese?"

"I should have asked this earlier," Della says. "Who's the best?"

That's always the first question and the right question: who's the best? Start at the best. You may say, "I can't afford it. They're too expensive." The best is always the least expensive, because they do it right the first time. They're the best because they do the most of it. If you have an operation for varicose veins, go to the guy who's done seven thousand, not the guy who just did one and botched it.

The doctor tells Della, "There's one who's the best. A chap up in Toronto."

"Good," she says. "Give me his name. Set it up. Call him up right now. I'm flying."

The next morning, on her own recognizance, she flies up to Toronto. The doctor comes in with six other docs who are going to watch the procedure.

Again, you don't want somebody bad-mouthing you. The doctor comes in and says, "Miss Reese, I'm a great fan of yours. I have every one of your gold records. I love your music. By the way, this operation's going to be a piece of cake."

Whom do you want to operate on you: somebody who says, "Will you please sign this, so you can't sue me after you're dead," or somebody who says, "This operation will be a piece of cake"?

"By the way, Miss Reese," the doctor went on, "if you don't get nauseous, you could watch this operation. There's only pain on the outside of the brain. We're going to put a topical anesthetic on it, and we're going to cut open your cranium. We're going to pull your brain out about five inches, do a little cutout and a little suturing, and there'll be no problem."

Della said, "I've always wanted to play doctor. That'd be hot. You mean I get to watch?"

"You get to watch."

She is now being operated on. Her brain is five inches outside of the body. She's looking in the mirror, and she says, "Doc, get somebody to get a tape recorder."

"Why?"

"Because I got the music in me. Somebody get a tape recorder, because I got my next gold record, and the reason you want it is that if, God forbid, this operation doesn't work, it's going to pay your fee."

In seconds, one of the assistants had a tape recorder, and that became her next gold record. You can't know when the ideas are going to magnetize you to your good. You've got to be ready always.

Another time, Della and I are doing an event here in Southern California. I take my wife's Volvo station wagon, which is loaded with stuff. We're going to have lots of folks. Della loves to have little kids come to her, because she is like my other hero, Lionel Richie, who always tests out his music on kids. If they dance and get into it, it's a taker. If they don't, it isn't.

Anyhow, Della says, "Bring your little babies, and they can sit in front of me." I come, and somehow during the day, I lose my wife's keys. She comes in my car, brings the kids. The kids have a good time with Della. We're ready to leave. She says, "Let's go." I tell my wife, "I can't find your keys."

"What are you going to do?" my wife said.

I go home to my office and go into deep meditation. I keep saying, "I'm the keys, I'm the keys" for twenty minutes.

All of a sudden, I go into freeze-frame, just as you do when you're playing tennis and you lock in it for a perfect hit. I see the keys on the third shelf of the kitchen of the convention center, even though I've never been in the room. It doesn't matter if you weren't there. Your subconscious knows everything.

Edgar Cayce and the Indians call it the Akashic records. It's God. It's infinite intelligence. It is the stuff of the universe. There are forty terms for it. It doesn't matter whether you know the them; it just matters that you know it exists.

I come back to the convention center. The keys are on the third shelf.

Once you know how to use your inner senses, you know how to give yourself the rewards from the end result. I had the keys before I'd gotten the keys.

Sylvester Stallone saw himself on the cover of *Time* magazine and *Sports Illustrated*. After *Rocky* was a hit, he was indeed on those covers.

Actor Paul Hogan is an ocker. That's a term that Australians apply to someone who's from the back country and has a thick accent. It's like saying you're from the ghetto, boy, and you're not going anywhere.

Although Hogan was ill-educated, he saw himself cutting it. He was a bridge painter for twelve years, painting the Sydney Harbour Bridge—which had all the romance and sex appeal of painting the Golden Gate Bridge—but he entertained his mates every day.

In Australia, they had their own version of *America's Got Talent*; it was called *Famous Faces in Australia*. His friends said, "Look, Paul. Why don't you go on, mate? You're really funny." He has no script, comes on, is brilliantly good.

His mastermind partner, the producer John Cornell, comes on and says, "I'm now your new partner. You're rough, raw, virgin talent. I can polish you, hone you, and make you spectacular." They shake hands on a 50-50 deal. They've never had a contract that hasn't been 50-50 on a handshake deal.

"What do you want to do?" Cornell asked Hogan.

"I want to get rid of Australia's down under image. I want people to see themselves as up over, no longer down under."

Hogan does a free commercial with the line, "G'day, mate. Put another shrimp on the barbie." He makes Australia the number one tourist destination. In two-minute vignettes, little mini-stories, he writes the script for the film *Crocodile Dundee*.

Have you seen *Crocodile Dundee*? In one scene, the hero is in New York with his beloved, and a guy comes up with a knife. Crocodile Dundee says, "That ain't no knife." He pulls out a Bowie knife and says, "*That's* a knife."

In the last scene, Crocodile Dundee is separated from his beloved, and he literally walks on the heads and hardhats and shoulders of New Yorkers to get toward her. If you have the right results or reasons you want, it doesn't matter what the appearance is. You'll get there.

Pink Baby Booties

When Patty and I got married, somebody asked us, "Do you want a boy or a girl?" she said without any equivocation, "I want a little daughter."

Her friend said, "Well, then, I'll knit you a pair of pink baby booties," which we hung at the head of our bed. It worked so well that we got two daughters.

One of our chiropractic friends said, "Have you read Frédérick Leboyer's book *Birth without Violence*? He says that in America, we're using the King Louis XIV method of child birthing, which is hard on women, and it's not nice. We throw the newborn kid upside down and spank them on the fanny, and then we cut the umbilical cord way too soon. It's much better if, when you take the baby out, you have music playing."

My friend Wally "Famous" Amos convinced me. He said, "Mark, when you go in, go in with a kazoo." Wally carries a kazoo everywhere.

So my daughter Melanie was also born with me playing the kazoo. Even at the age of one, she played the kazoo beautifully, and she's got great musical talent.

Kids can hear two weeks before they're born. They're saying, "I'm not leaving; there's an idiot out there. I've been in the hot water bed nine months. It's a little cramped in the quarters now, but things might expand." Ultimately they have to have a C-section.

Leboyer taught, "Give the baby a birthing bath." He also said, "Don't take off all the vernix"—the white, cheeselike substance that's found on newborns—"because it keeps the person from having wrinkles for the rest of their life."

When my daughter Elizabeth and, later, my other daughter, Melanie, were born, we had an interface through our heart chakras. Those were the highest, most joy-filled, and most rapturous experiences of my being. It's never been better. It's the exalted moment. It's what Kahlil Gibran says in *The Prophet*: you can fall in love as deeply in one second as you can in a lifetime. It doesn't matter that you've been hanging out for eighteen hours and you've see lots of pain and anguish and tears. You go through it and you get to the other side, because you started knowing that you're going to have a wondrous miracle called life.

Let me add this one little idea: you've got to have an attitude of gratitude. You've got to be thankful in advance.

There's No Time

As a quick review, go into relaxed awakeness, controlled reverie; get into the theater of your mind. See your life the way you want to see it to the exclusion of the way you don't want to see it. Function from the end result. Emotionalize the reality in a positive rather than a negative way. Sense it with your five interior senses to match your five exterior senses.

Give yourself rewards. If the rewards are good enough, you can do anything. If somebody's got a gun to your head and you're only going to live if X happens, you'll figure out how to get X done. If you've got to earn more money in less time than you've ever done, you'll figure out how to do it. Parkinson's law says that time expands or contracts based on the mental paradigm that we've put on. I've used this technology to contract time.

At one time I'm up in Pasco, Florida. I've got an hour and a half to get to the airport. I'm sitting with an associate at lunch. We're enjoying it so much that time evaporates, and I've got a half-hour to get there. He has a Lamborghini outside. I said, "I know you're fast, and I know this thing can fly, but I need to keep my physical body intact."

"You believe in thought projection," he said, "Let's close our eyes, meditate, and we'll be there in exactly twenty-eight minutes." I don't know exactly how the time warp worked, but we arrived in exactly twenty-eight minutes. I walked onto the plane with elegance and dignity.

"There is no time or space," as Einstein said, "Man created time so everything wouldn't all happen now, and he created space so everything wouldn't all happen here."

The Hands of Christ

Let me conclude with one little story. Back during World War II, it was the promise of all the military not to wipe out churches. That's why the Vatican never got hit, despite heavy bombing all around it.

Unfortunately, in northern Italy our army didn't have good ballistics or logistics, and they wiped out a church. The war's over. The soldiers won't come home for another three months. They're living with the Italians—wonderful, robust people that believe in *abbondanza*. They've welcomed the troops into their homes and hearts.

The Americans meet with the citizenry and say, "We've inadvertently wiped out this church. We're really apologetic; we didn't mean to. It is unfortunate, but we'd like to work with your citizenry to rebuild it."

They rebuild the church so that it's better than before. Out in front, there was a Carrara marble statue that stood seven feet, six inches tall; it was called the *Christos*, the Christ statue. They put it all back together and polished it. They made it beautiful, but the statue was missing its hands.

Our soldiers and the citizenry got together and said, "This is a great statue. Should we put on false hands, or should we leave Christ without hands?"

They decided it would be better to put a plaque in front, and here's what it said: "Christ's only hands are yours. Christ's only mind is yours. Christ's only heartbeat is yours."

May you use your mind power and your visualization to take you into the exalted moment so as to become all you can become, because spirits hands, mind and heart, as stated above, are yours!

Seven

Creative Visualization

This is a creative visualization exercise. You can do it in several ways: you can read it and do each part of the sequence as you go along; you can have someone else read it to you; or you can record it, say, on your phone, and listen as you play it back.

For best results be in a relaxed position in your bed, on the floor, or in your favorite chair. Be comfortable.

Create a space of relaxed, uninterrupted awakeness. Close your eyes and repeatedly internalize these thoughts to yourself:

I close my outer eyes, and I open my inner eyes. I breathe deeply and fully, with every atom of my being and exhale any fear, doubt, indecision, pain, and procrastination. All that is out, out, out. I inhale love and joy. I inhale just a little bit more to let the breath penetrate my whole life. I exhale anything that is not loving and joyous.

I resume breathing. I tilt my inner eyes up at a forty-five-degree angle. In my mind's eye, I see the theater of my imagination. I open up the curtains. I am watching a play of my own creation called *Me*.

I have the remote control in my hand. I can click the channel and change what's on the screen of my space. By sowing new thoughts, I reap new experiences. I have infinite options available to me.

I'm clicking the channel. I'm looking at a new me, a radiant me, a self-confident me, a me with resolute self-reliance. I feel good about me at every atom of my being. My eyes shine; my skin radiates. I have a healing touch. People get better around me.

People get close to me, and they feel better. I love *me* at the depth of my being. I am in the sacred sanctuary of my mind. I look at myself on the screen of my imagination, and I declare it's good and very, very, good. I see myself as I want to be. I manifest my heart's desire.

I know exactly what I want. I have it written down on paper. More importantly, I have it imprinted in my mind. The picture is clear; it's in Technicolor. I hear the right words coming out of all the actors called my life. The main actor is the sweetheart of my life, who plays a significant and important and totally supportive role.

My family members are now coming to me one at a time. If they have said anything harsh, cruel, demeaning, or dehumanizing to me, I alone have the power, in the exalted moment, to edit everything. I hear new words come out. The caress on my ear sweetens the feel of my mind. I increase the love I have for myself and the love I have for them and all the experiences we share.

Life for me is not a dress rehearsal, but I live in the home entertainment center called my mind. I have the ability in the instant to edit, add to, rewrite, script my life the way I want. Wow. I'm looking good. I am feeling good. I'm feeling good to my toes, so good, so alive, so vital.

My knees move in harmony with the music of the universe. I am healthy throughout my midsection. Every beat of my heart is clicking to higher levels of help—high-level ones, spiritual beings, bountiful, abundant, overflowing, ever-flowing prosperity. My face exudes God's countenance of joy, the emana-tions of life. They're so good. I'm doing well while I'm doing good.

I love my life and every aspect of it, every nuance, every facet. It feels good. I live in faith and love more fully every day. I am living in the excited fabric called my teacher that I've created in the sweet here and now of consciousness.

I realize my visualizations are causal. I'm making up my life in my mind, and I'm making it really good. I'm good at making up what I want. I'm good at seeing it. I'm good at feeling it. I'm good at believing it. I'm good at expecting it. I'm good at recognizing and realizing all the good that I desire. I now produce a definite feeling state that I want to emerge to produce my highest, loftiest, noblest, and most aspired realizations of health, happiness, wealth, love, and the discovery of new solutions.

That's right. I am the solutions of my problems, and nobody else is. I communicate them crystal clear inside me. I deploy them on paper. I see ideas come to me. Then exactly the right people show up that need to hear these solutions, that can energize them, exercise them, manifest them, realize them to the greater good of myself, themselves, and the world.

I live a life of dedicated purposefulness. I am clearly on purpose. I know my life's purpose, and I write it down regularly. I eagerly communicate to those with willing, listening, interested ears. I live and I love my body. I dress with a vibrant flair. It makes my heart sing, because it's so clear.

I know what to do and how to do it, because it's in writing. When people make requests of me, I look toward my purpose. I can instantly declare whether participating in their activity is on purpose or off purpose for me. If it's on purpose, I say thank you very much; I'll help, I'll participate, I'll assist from the depth of my being. If it's off purpose, I say thank you for sharing; it doesn't fit me.

Because my mind has that clarity, I'm going to higher ground along with other people. They're waking up to the lightness of being.

I was born to visualize and realize new possibilities for myself, my family, my associates, my city, my country, my world, and my universe. I've seen possibilities for a life lived fully. I no longer limit myself to living one life in a lifetime.

I know that the inner spaces of my mind can run on many lines and channels simultaneously. Once I push the start button, I keep unfolding pictures in my mind.

I own the decisive quality that says stop or go in my mind, and I'm hitting all the green lights in my mind. I see it, I feel it. I believe it at the depth of my very being. I am supported and sourced in wondrous new ways by those who surround me and are singing the same songs. My heart is singing. They're attracted to me. They're growing as I am. They're becoming like me. They are wayshowers; they are lamplighters. Their candles, like mine, are lit, resonating, glowing, and taking in light, where previously there was darkness. Others tilt their wicks towards mine and towards the ones of those that I associate with and light them. Everyone resonates to the same tingling vibration. They light the ones to their sides in turn. Everyone's candle is lit, and there's a roar, glow, joyous, resonating, in the chime of life, and new birth is there.

This new world makes me awake to things I was asleep to previously, because in some ways I feel like a rebellious teenager. I want to burst out of my skin into the unlimited beingness, the unlimited greatness, the unlimited totality, and wonder of the universes.

In my visualization, I can do that. My imagination is unbounded. I feel like a little child exuding joy and being happy, happy, happy. Independence of spirit is my lofty goal. I claim I am free. I am free. I choose to be awake to the fact that I'm free. I'm free to be who I really am and who I want to be, and to choose whom I want to be with. I'm free to do what I want, because I want as much as I want. I'm free of pain, injury, and conflict.

My mind is in harmony. I align myself with other beings who want it all. I am free to move fully and drink fully of all of the good that life has in it.

I'm experiencing joyful workability in all my relationships. My relationships are luminous, a wonder, a joy, nurturing, satisfying, in ways that are mutual, personal, and extrapersonal. Together we grow and glow.

I now have enormous abilities to get along with others. I have enormous abilities to make my own life work, to make my lifestyle work for myself and others. My environment is clicking where it had been falling apart. I'm putting it back together in new and better ways.

I'm taking the divinity of my stewardship seriously. I take accountability and responsibility to act in accordance with the greater good, the greater God. I am making my world work. Whatever is in ashes, I am becoming the phoenix that rises and flies and soars in miraculously effective ways. As this phoenix floats overhead, I see what needs to be done. I know how to do it, and I know how to deal with it. I bring into my environment those that want to do it with me, those that have passion in their very souls.

While I'm doing this, I enjoy the simple pictures. I am in harmonic balance. I am not a workaholic;

I'm a joyaholic. I live in the exulted moment of play, work, and spiritual beingness. I live fully in every present moment. My mind automatically organizes what I need to know, who I need to be, what I need to be, and all that I need to have before I even request it. My mind automatically sequences multiple priorities so they get done and click in harmony. My nature is to be creative, open, and caring, and I have a passionate desire for growth at all levels.

I joyfully choose to contribute at new, higher levels to myself and to all I come in contact with. I now contribute vibrations to all people alive and all the people coming on our little spaceship.

I choose to grow in wisdom. I am wise in deep and profound manners. The wisdom of Solomon is mine. I revel in new wisdom. The love that exists in the universe is mine. Infinite love is mine to have, to hold, to behold, to befriend, to share in the every atom of my being. I feel love into very small caresses of my thoughts, the wink of my eye, the way I look, the way I feel.

I feel new levels of some poise and elegance. For the universe, I see centropy, things coming together at higher and higher levels. I know the universe's compensatory balancing system is always in replete balance. If the teeter-totter tilts one way, my thinking can help it tilt back into balance. I find centropy where there was entropy. I heal the scar and make it a new, bright, luminescent star.

My power to grow increases at each moment; I can see it with my inner eye. I hold it with the string of love and fervor of all the saints, of all the angels. I automatically produce the same things, and life sparkles, shines, and exudes in greatness. It feels good and very, very, very good.

Love is my normal, natural state of being. Environments I walk into are biologically oriented. They have lots of plants. They have plants that feel my vibrations and express more life and emit more pheromones. The environment smells better because I've entered it. The vibratory rate of all people in all races makes them better off when they get close to me, whether they know my state of being as present or not.

I am moved. I am loving, and I help. People love it. I love to be loved by people of love. I attract loving people into my experiences—those that hear of this love, awaken to it, and discover its dawning realization for themselves. It's like walking on a beach in Hawaii and watching the sunlight over the turquoise Pacific. It's mystical, and it's shining.

Light warms my being. When it hits the mirror called *me*, it radiates love to all the beings in the world. The words "I love you, I love you, I love you" are oft heard from my lips. I praise others. I love them nonverbally, because I love myself and I can love them. Then I get them into the state where they love themselves. They can open to be 100 percent loving.

I am now in the state of high healthfulness. It is normal and natural for me to be in a state of high level of beingness, no matter what my age is. I'm getting better, for I know that my spirit is immortal, and it dances to the command of my own words. My words are made flesh, and I claim that I am lovely, and I live in a healthy way always and always. I'm healthy in my mind and in my body. I'm healthy in my spirit. I think, feel, and see myself acting in healthy ways. I hang around people who nourish me correctly and nurture the soul of my being.

I generate healthy thoughts. They come back to me and have me propagate even healthier thoughts. I am self-replenishingly healthy. I generate health from the core of my being, no matter what I've heard, what I've thought, what I've felt, or what I've been told. I am healthy. I am truly and divinely healthy. I am healthy at all levels. I am healthy in my affairs.

In my creative visualizations, I eradicate, I renounce, I disintegrate things I don't feel good about. I look at them and say goodbye. Now I'm in high-level healthfulness. I am committed to my well-being and to that of all those who surround me—family, associates, fellow citizens, and coastronauts on Spaceship Earth.

In my visualizations, I ask for what I want, and I get it. I get everything I want, need, and desire, and I'm living in my highest and best. I only use my power of visualization for good and for the good of others. I hear others compliment me and my great, grand, amazing contributions.

Finally, I am now fully empowered, and I see myself giving away empowerment to others. I manage year in and year out to increase my salary, earnings, and dividends. Every part of my life is fun. I am happy. I am using my resources, talents, and abilities in ever greater waves. I see a bright future for myself and everyone else, and so it is. I'm delighted, and I'm excited about it.

Thank you. Thank you. Thank you.

CPSIA information can be obtained
at www.ICGtesting.com
Printed in the USA
JSHW041949271020
9156JS00006B/41